Collected Poems

of

Raymond Souster

Volume One

1940-55

Book design by Michael Macklem

Printed in Canada

PUBLISHED IN CANADA BY OBERON PRESS

This book is for Lia, as always,
for Louis and Irving,
and for the memory of John Sutherland .

Never be Finished; In Love; Shediac Blues; Puppets; Apart; The Unbreakable; Gone; Lovers, Dominion Square; Reserve; On a Dock in St. John; Falling of the Acorns; Portrait of Elinor; Second Meeting; Together Again; Need of an Angel; Sunnyside Amusement Park; Happy New Year; Night Watch; Girl Asleep; Shake Hands with the Hangman; Yonge Street Saturday Night; Our Night; Nocturnal; The Nest; On the Brown Bed of our Choosing; It is Becoming Grey Now; Dreams were Always Cheap; Yorkshire Village; These Words, this Music; Trees After Rain; Poem for a Snapshot; Friday Night; Print of the Sandpiper.

The Highway; When I See Old Men; A Dream of Hanlan's; Bar, Harlem; Speakers, Columbus Circle; City Hall Street; Times Square; Riverdale Zoo; Man Dying; Lambton Riding Woods; Brant Place; In Praise of Loneliness; Court of General Sessions.

Lagoons, Hanlan's Point; Summer's Girls; Scoudouc: that Lost Year; Lights and Shadows; The Twenty-Fifth of December; Self-Portrait from the Year 1952; O Mighty River; Roller-Skate Man; The Man who Finds that his Son has Become a Thief; Litter of the Late Last Rose; Steel Plant Saturday Night; Salute to Bobby Hackett; The Lilac Poem; Freak Show; Coal Piles, Ashbridge's Bay; Afternoon by the Ouse; Storm in November; To an Anti-Semite; London Rendezvous; Memo to the Human Race.

Jazz Concert, Massey Hall; Death of the Dawn Patrol; Softly as First Leaves Fall; Icicle Outside the Barracks; Sleep Toronto; Let Me Always Remember; Question for a Soldier; Three Ways of Looking at New York; I Watched a Bird; Troopship

the Oxford Hotel; Amusement Park; The Opener; Jeanette; Along the Danforth; High Dive; Red Fruit; The Bowling Alley; Our Gun-Armourer Corporal; Prisoner of the State, 1951; On Grenadier Pond; Summer's Flood; The Train Past Auschwitz; Cid's Poem; One of our Young Soldiers, Drunk, Spends his First Night in Brussels; Fredericton; Club Night; Rag-and-Bones-Man; St. Mary's Street: 3 AM; The Snapshot from Mallorca; Drunk, on Crutches; Hanlan's Point Amusement Park; A Letter from Mallorca; First Spring Workout; VD Instruction, RCAF; Civil Defence; The Angel of Christmas; Downtown TV Aerial; Reversal; The Rainbow; Old Man Leaning on a Fence; Red Berries; Little Mag.

Poetry Reading; A Bed Without a Woman; Two Dead Robins; The Collector; Gran Via; Battle Jacket; Centre Island, Late September; Charlie; Evening in the Suburbs; The Miracle; The Literary Life; Put it on Record; The Monkey, the Organ-Grinder; Yonge Street Re-Opening; Volleys; Again the Sandwich-Board Man; No Escape; The Voyage; Sixteen Grenville Street; First Spring Day in the Canyons; First Day of the World Series; The Bar and the All-Night Mission; Taking the Cure; The Changes; Mira Night; The Fire in the Tenement; Madonna of the Lunch-Counter; Viewers; The Faces of the Crowd; The Bat that Came in One Night; World Traveller at Twenty-One; British Liberation Army; The Negro Girl; The Difference; Bottles; Your Absence; Death by Streetcar; The Child and the Snow; The New Fence; Girl at the Corner of Elizabeth and Dundas; Litter; The Winter Overcoat; Egg-Shell Blue; Dead Squirrel; Pin Boy at the Old Bowling Alley; The Red Sash; What Can I Say; The Mating Season; The Kinder Decision; Flight of the Roller-Coaster; Civic Reception; The Ugliest Woman; The Toy Ladder; Man on the Beach; Writers' Conference; The Recollection; This Skull-Capped Priest; The Uncouth Poem; The New Mattress.

PREFACE

This is the first volume in a projected four-volume edition of my *Collected Poems 1940–1980*. It contains all the verse from the period 1940 to 1955 that I wish to retain in print. For the first time these poems will appear in a single volume in the order in which they were originally published.

I should hasten to add that many of the earliest poems were written slightly before 1940 (from 1938 on), but 1940 was for me such a special year that I have decided to bend the limits of chronology to that extent. It was in 1940 that I had my first few acceptances by small American publications of the new "social" poetry I was attempting to write. That was also the year I made a largely unconscious but long-range commitment to poetry. For much the same reason this volume begins with poems completed by 1940 which did not appear until late in 1944 in the anthology *Unit of Five*.

The book ends with selections from a mimeographed booklet entitled *For What Time Slays*, which appeared in 1955. Another similar mimeographed collection, *Walking Death*, also appeared in that year, but because of space limitations it will appear as the opening group of poems in the second volume, which is scheduled for publication next year.

I have taken advantage of this new and definitive edition of my work to revise where it seemed necessary, strictly adhering, however, to the original intent of each poem. In addition, over fifty poems that have never before been published in book form have been chosen to round out the collection.

RAYMOND SOUSTER

Unit of Five
(1944)

THE FOND DESIRE

Night on the city again:
the hurrying, branching crowds
with laughing faces, hearts in the heavens,
that quiet-eating acid despair
etching many other faces, the hearts in darkness.

O God, I call down a curse on loneliness
in any breath tonight drinking in this spring air.
Let pain's jagged needle be forever shattered
in a thousand pieces: let love, let peace,
though unearned, though foreign in these gates,
wing back, surge over this sky with a roar of gladness
no squadron of bombers could match
shaking deep at her iron heart.

LATE MARCH

Almost impossible to think of,
to comprehend—the words war, bombings, air-raid shelters—
with this afternoon sun glowing spring-like,
with the dry, cheerful voices of the sparrows.

A sun that sends a warmth like peace
flooding over the roof-tops, lashing out at windows,
a live mountain stream with that innocence
born of highlands, kept virginal still in those cities
reverberating with madness, with destruction.

And though I know the sun's a liar, an escapist,
who are you, O world, that he should favour this dunghill
with light from the skies shining-clear and piercing as truth?

13

REQUEST

The band mustn't stop now, even if it's well after one,
the dance must flow on till two, even three o'clock,
the beat strong and even, saxes low and sweet,
no low-down jive from the horns. Keep turning that sheet
    music over,
keep playing the same numbers through if you have to,
send out for more beer if you feel your thirst can't stand the
    strain,
but keep playing, boys . . .
                      give each one here at least another hour
of pleasure before that world outside, ugly, dark,
claims them, calls them, lines them up again;
if this is only a dream a dream is something, anyway,
not too much, admitted, but still so much more
than those machines would grant, those time-clocks allow,
a dream of happy times, of unruffled peace
that their fathers bungled, somehow lost,
their grandfathers left unwritten in their wills.

So give them their little dream, boys,
keep the beat even, saxes sweet, soft and low,
horns muted, caressing.

14

NIGHT OF RAIN

Rain on the streets: go ahead, make up your little poem
about wet boughs and the silver sandals
of the rain: it's still one hell of a night,

and the old men on the Queen Street pavements
won't bum any cigarettes, the boys and girls on these other
    streets won't bloom
like any spring flowers tangled in dark rotted weeds,
while that tortuous stream of life that never ends, never ends,
along the pus-lines of this, my city,

will cage itself in the four trapped walls
of furnished and unfurnished rooms,
waiting for this night to go,

this night to go, this darkness of their lives.

15

END OF THE DAY

Now they crowd into elevators and descend
to streets where fresh air, the noise of traffic
bring these faces alive. Faces released
for a few hours of play and sleep
before alarums jangle and the game resumes,
leaving behind the stained front of banks, trusts, corporations,
along with the lifeless air, dust settling silently
on board-room furniture, along endless corridors,

where now a poison gas from the death-smells
of profit and loss, credits, margins, cash flow,
will hunt out any rats in their holes,
kill them painlessly one by one.

TEN PM

Invisible hands are washing uncounted dishes,
the clink of plates jarring together
tinkles the darkness in soot-blackened alleys.
The junkmen going through their last tired motions
in the cans overflowing with garbage treasure,
hear the sound, and the thought of food
runs like a sore in their numbed minds. The eyes grope,
the hands reach down into the cans again. . . .

O westward the lights stretch, paling diamonds
far and further into the night-time,
the lake beside them shuddering softly to the moon-touch.
But the stars are colder, crueler here
where the pavement shudders when streetcars rumble over,
where the flares of neon flick their fiery anger
at the idiot postures of black-hearted buildings,
where the rancid smoke downcurls and settles
in nose, in mouth, in fissures of the heart.

HUNGER

After you've laid the quarter down and had a meal,
wiped your mouth with a paper napkin, then walked out of
    the quick lunch,
head higher, heart lighter, body somehow stronger, simply
    because you've eaten,
because you've done again what people do when they feel
    hungry,

how long will you walk on air, how long will you smile at the
    world,
before you remember what a man with empty pockets always
    remembers,
always fears, sometimes goes almost crazy remembering,

as night comes on, as the streets become dark and cold,
and you are alone with the sound of your feet on the pavements,
that pain there again in your belly, a thousand tiny needles
    jabbing, jabbing,

how long will you go on panhandling like the blind man on
    the corner,
how much more of this can you take before you steal, before
    you maim, before you kill?

SEARCH

Not another bite, not another cigarette,
or a final cup from the coffee-urn before you leave
the warmth steaming right to the windows
of this hamburger joint where the Wurlitzer
booms all night without a stop,
where the onions are thick between the buns.

Wrap yourself well in that cheap coat that holds out the wind
    like a sieve,
you have a long way to go, the streets are dark,
and you may have to wander all night before you find
another heart quite so lonely, so nearly mad with boredom,
so filled with such strength, such tenderness of love.

19

NIGHT-TOWN

These ferret eyes may look from the cellars,
the shabby, the hungry take heart.
Now you may walk these streets, have no look upon you,
no searchlight sun to blast and betray your pride.
Emerge from the tavern door, stagger into the shadows,
no-one will laugh or call the waggon;
stand and give the boys the come-on,
they will think you young and attractive in the darkness.

City, while the night rides high,
the stink, the filth is forgotten,
what the sewers run with, what the hospitals throw in the
    garbage,
what the stockyard breathes, is transformed as if by magic
into the white necks, multiplying mirrors, glittering
    encores,
while the buildings climb with a grandeur they do not possess,
winds blow with a freshness they do not keep
when the dawn comes, when the sun breaks up,
when the light of day blinds with its accusation.

20

REALITY

The glow of the restaurant is faked,
the dream of the movie is blown like an insubstantial cloud
in the street again, and what is real is the traffic's not loud
but more a muffled, insinuating scream,
the raw wind that whips and clutches at papers and bites
at the old grey flanks of buildings, and a man who stands
mind blank to perfumed amours, cabarets, weekends,
all our carefully planned civilized delights,
holding a box of shoe-laces in unendingly shaking hands.

O YOUNG MEN O YOUNG COMRADES

(With apologies to Stephen Spender)

O young men O young comrades
it's too late now to leave those houses
your fathers built for your weekend drinking parties,
your sexual horseplay; much too late
for even a bicarbonate.
                                Rather you should count
those fabulous possessions which begin with your fat gut and
    dirty mind,
not forgetting the dandruff caked in your scalp, the muscles
    untrained
for anything except your careless heat.

O young men O young comrades
it's much too late now to leave your great houses
where the people with class drop in—
the stock- and bond-men biting through their dollar cigars,
the daughters of millionaires lighted up with cascades of
    diamonds.

O comrades, when you leave your smooth drinks, soft
    chesterfields,
slip into the sportscar and zoom out, certain of a sure thing,
all the way give your engine hell and don't forget
what waits for you downtown was never dead man's meat.

THE ENEMIES, THE HATED

What do they care for a book,
would they ever read a chapter through or a verse
without yawning, do you ever think they could stand

before a painting and really enjoy it
without something lewd to catch their eye
or something not understood right away to be laughed at,
do you think they give a damn how you eat your heart out,
kill yourself quickly or slowly, how you finally go mad?

You are not of *their* world, you are strangers,
the enemies, the hated,
because you have dared to laugh at their money,
their women, the hollow cheapness of their lives,

because they cannot laugh off, cannot pay off,
the epitaph you have written.

TO THE CANADIAN POETS, 1940

Come, my little eunuchs, my tender virgins,
it's high time you were home and in bed.
The wind's cold and strong in the streets now,
and it's almost ten o'clock.

Soon whores will be obvious at corners,
and I wouldn't want you accosted or given the eye;
soon drunks will be turned out of beverage rooms
and you could be rolled or raped up a dark lane.

So quickly find your houses, turn the latch-key, set the night-
    lock,
remember to dress with the blinds down. Then safe in bed you
    may dream
of Pickthall walking hand in hand with her fairies,
of Lampman turning his back on Ottawa.

24

THE INVADERS

Crickets repeat themselves
in the grass, the road is darkness, and shadows bulge
as our headlights guide us safely home.

As we return from the smalltown movie
to dark trees underneath our windows,
to the peace of this farm that drugs us like opium

to the madman radio, concentration camps,
bombings of civilians, those reported missing,
today's hidden terror, tomorrow's open outrage.

These are all so far from horses, cows,
the colour of hay on distant fields . . .

but moving slowly, closer to the heart,
closer to fear, to death, to agony without a name.

EVEN A WORM WILL TURN, GENTLEMEN

Even a worm will turn, gentlemen. . . .

Nothing can suffer, nothing can endure better than a worm,
but even such a humble creature will at last grow tired
of rot, of corruption, of decay,
no matter how entrenched, how powerful; even a worm
may demand more than blindness,
a prouder, swifter movement than crawling;

even a worm is aware
that slavery has never equalled life,
fear never equalled happiness.

Even a worm will turn, gentlemen. . . .

(You wouldn't believe this simple act of turning
could heave like a hundred earthquakes, cut like a thousand
    swords, roar like ten thousand bombers,
straight at the heart, the still centre,
of a world whirling with a tired flame!)

26

AIR RAID

(Madrid 1937)

Bombs have laid these houses
open to the sky. The dead face the sun
directly from their stretchers, no fear now
in the eyes, nothing there but blackness
where once life sparkled, love swelled.

High above, still gloating, the hate-crossed vultures
sniff the smell of blood, the smoke of ruin.
They hum with fresh purpose,
their black wings glistening in the morning air,
as other slick droppings of murder
fall shrieking from their stinking bowels.

REPLY

Is there really much more to say?
Won't the closing of a door, a face lost around a corner,
the sun's last gold, the falling of a voice on air,
speak the remaining necessary words
and leave no anger, bitterness, regret?

If there's much more than that to be said
it had better be left unspoken,
it had better be left for the wind at your window to explain,
the wind that blows the smoke, the rain, everything away in
     time.

SOME NIGHT

It all comes back,
terribly,
some night you are alone,
sitting at a window,
looking out at dark-green trees,
hearing the night wind
sift freshly through their branches.

Yes, it all comes back,
all of it—
wasted days, cheap talk,
childish acts, empty bravado—
that you live by,
that you use like weapons
to protect the soft yielding skin
of your little world. . . .

Yes, it comes back terribly,
it repeats and repeats in your mind
till you can't drive the thought away
that it would be better if it all were ended,

because you'll never catch any meaning, any moment,
that the morning won't show up
like fake jewels in the daylight,
and that there'll always be
cheaters to break your faith,
liars to mock every word,
whores to make you puke
on that love undying.

COMMUNICATION TO THE ENEMY

So young, yet they've managed to put a limp into our walk,
so strong, yet our arms are either tied or lopped off neatly
    at the shoulder,
so brave, yet our minds are harshly horizoned to the teeth of
    their wire.

And still they're not content but are out with hound and gun,
searching to destroy any fire left burning in our hearts,
that precious, ardent flame.

Then let us tell them all that our trails are cold,
the fugitives more numerous than first reported missing,
with always comrades, hope, waiting beyond the border. . . .

THE WARNING

How strong is the fist
that strikes them down, that never lets them lift
their heads up for one unguarded look
at the sky, at the world beyond
the dark definition of roofs,
the dust laid on the pavements.

Yet in many eyes, like the cold hard light from tombs
bound for centuries to harbour darkness,
I read a hatred more passionate than any lover's
wild words to the moon; more noble than all
the unsung regiments suffering the whims of generals
in murderous drumfires: without any of that blindness.

So now I'll give a warning to that fist, that merciless arm,
shout it out in the streets night and morning:
they only save their words, build up their hate,
waiting for that sinister shadow of a hand
to fall again: this time to fall forever!

Direction
(1943-46)

NADA

To smile the right smile at the right girls passing by in just
    the right manner,
to follow up your advantage with the right technique at the
    exact precise moment,
to act the well-known cutting-in-with-such-apparent-ease
    Romeo of all the local dance-joints,
to be the funniest, craziest, most sought after, adored pet of the
    small-talk afternoon tea circles, the midnight smoke-draped
    hangover parties,
to force with such expert hands the heat of our virgin of last
    year but one only till she moans for deliverance on the
    softly lighted chesterfield scene,
to drive the newest, shiniest, longest, most-cylindered of the
    latest models down the four-lane highway, bound for
    supper club or weekend summer hotel,

this is to live, this is to meet each moment of each day with
    the maximum prescribed measure of enjoyment,
this is to be alive, this is truly, truly to melt into the heart-beat,

or if it isn't, wise guy,
what else is there, what better pattern have you to offer in its
    place,
what better way have you to suggest to kill the slow slow hours
    of the day, the slower, even longer hours of the night,
what do you offer, what am I bid, or do I hear any takers?—
    going, going, gone—
sold to the gentleman with the empty face, the broken mind,
    to the girl with no arms, no mouth, no breasts and the eyes
    of a serpent.

FOR YOU

I

As many ways as they have to say wonderful
I could rave about you—but why should I bother
to tell people anything?—they never helped find you,
and sometimes I think they did all they could
to hurt us and kill what we carried in our hearts.

But then I feel sorry
for the whole stupid lot of them
with their dirty rotten lives,
and I want to give them
a glimpse of heaven, so I write a poem
with you lying in a room,
and let them come up to its window,
look in at your proud loveliness.

2

The cat in this house curls up
all her cinnamon lissome length
on the chair, and I run my fingers
over her pliant, furry body,
then watch how the nervous tail twitches,
how the eyes and the ears move together
as she feels my loving caress.

So I allow myself this deception
(though even a cat should be told)
that I'm conjuring up you and the treasure
of your body soft as a kitten
snuggled close in beside me, dreaming still of your lips
that bite more quickly, more sharply
than cat's teeth along my fingers. . . .

3

O everywhere I went last night I thought of you.
When I went to the grill at the corner
I thought of you and me getting off
the streetcar at your corner, going into
the same restaurant where we'd sat
so many times at the back and spooned
our marshmallow sundaes:

                              then when I strolled
in the downtown streets through the crowds,
I thought of the two of us
coming out of Massey Hall that night
after the ballet, walking very close together up Yonge Street,
heads still spinning with the whirling movements of dancers,
    colours, music,

34

and feeling our love to be that same mad, spinning thing....
O darling, I looked at almost every face in the crowd,
hoping to see yours like some drunken, crazy man,
but after a while I couldn't stand it any longer,
had to walk home alone in the dark streets,
my hands held stiffly at my sides so empty, so lonely,
without yours like warm gloves to fit themselves to mine,
my heart heavier, damper than the night air
without the promise of your body's touch to send its fire
blazing up through all of me, a sparkling wine
always staggering my poor, poor head....

THE SNAKES

The snow falls, kills the grass,
the wind blows, takes the living heart from everything.

But you can't blame the snow
you can't blame the wind   .
you can't blame anything

any more than I blame you
for not being here beside me in the darkness
of this room where I feel the snakes,
the smooth snakes of loneliness,
winding their slithering coils round and round about me....

35

FALSE SPRING

No flowers bloom now between barrack-blocks,
the brown grass accents the lifelessness
of our days, at times more desperate
than the bloodless face of a slum child.
It's the only glittering promise
of warm spring winds advancing
down the roads of the camp, the rough-piercing brilliance
of the sun in our dull eyes that hint of any change
in the unbroken sternness of our season.

The mind suddenly dreams of lilies, Easter parades
on the Sunnyside boardwalk, that carnival of colour
unleashed on the bodies of women, long afternoons
in the parks, and nights that end
with walking to bed through sleepy, stone-darkened streets. . . .

But only the wind blowing hard at the window
of this barrack-room is real, that and the capricious sunshine
now in the Nova Scotia sky, and so the dreams
are brushed away again now, suddenly, angrily.

36

DECEPTION

Someone comes into the barrack-room
from the night outside, wet blobs of snow
sepulchre-white on the sombre blue
of his winter greatcoat.

The wind howls around these buildings
like a man chased hard by death,
but this room that is also my prison
changes into something warm, almost bright,
with the endless talk, the horseplay of the boys
stretched on their bunks, leaning against rough tables,
somehow close, somehow natural, even good,

with my whole world transformed, all at once becoming
a young girl's beautiful body,
all its ugly scars very well hidden
beneath her scarlet-flowing cape.

37

WITH SPRING

With spring
with the unfolding bud
with the shouts of children,
with the eyes of young men
following the slender legs of girls,

begins again
a rising chorus of death,
rained bombs, defiled bodies,
boyish hearts turned to steel
with the plunge of a tiger.

A hand goes up with a knife in it
to gash the red heart of the world.

You madmen
you baby killers
you pimps of this Christ.

38

EASTER, 1943

A little child
who knows no better
urinates by the wall
on the Easter lilies.

White lilies
snow princesses.

While a new generation of Christs
hammer unheeded from the tomb.

BALM

Although being people we must move among people,
comfort and help them as they also
must help and comfort us,

there are times when we grow very tired
of every face on the street,
men too much like animals,
women strangely lewd,
children the deliberate errors of their parents.

Then I move my hands lovingly over your curled-up body
as tenderly as I can, press all my fears, my petty hatreds
into the welcoming compassion of your lips.

Later we shall walk out laughing
into the lonely crowds.

NIGHT TRAIN LEAVING MONTREAL

This is the end of the earth.
This is nothingness.

No human moves or breathes
under this darkness.

Ghostly bridges, faded yellow lights,
long bridges of terror,
dim evil souls of the lights.

And water, smell of oil
like death from the dark water.

What dies here never lived.
What is to be born
waits an uncertain morning.

40

I WONDER IF OUR BOYS TONIGHT
ARE THINKING OF BOUCHARD'S DISMISSAL

These streets are warm tonight,
everyone out for a stroll, going somewhere,
lots of beer in the taverns,
plenty of fine food in restaurants.

Now the newsboys are shouting headlines,
and I buy a paper, thinking
maybe the Yanks took Cherbourg
or our boys are farther inland. . . .

But I forgot for a moment,
if only for a moment,
that I'm in Montreal
where they don't care about the War,
I forgot I'm in Canada
where they still don't know what war is. . . .

O Canada
my home my native land

so lucky there are still thousands
of young men willing to die for you
without knowing or caring why.

GOOD RAIN

It's raining, not shells
but grey sheets of rain,
and the green things of earth grow,
are life-shining, beautiful,
instead of dying
or being dead,
painted over with that blackness.

I walk in the rain,
feeling such goodness wash over my face, my arms,
praising this too-seldom whim.

VILLAGE BY THE SEA

Sometimes it gets so peaceful
you can almost hear
the dip of a bird's wing,
with the little houses so huddled together
you wonder if this isn't the place God came from.

But then those bells start ringing
in the big white church on the hill,
and up the road a crowd staggers, carrying in their hands
the chains of their birthright: while the idiots
beat their heads against the walls of the crazy house
as the miners coming off the shift
blink once at the light and go on
in darkness to their miserable hutches.

THE COLD EYE OF MORNING

What we felt last night is a different story today,
what we did last night may never happen again.
The darkness hides, the darkness lies,
but the cold eye of morning doesn't pull any punches.

We have our ways to go and we will go them.
Of course if we ever meet
we can shake hands, inquire about friends.

THE CITY

Who knows
the next gust of wind may tangle in your feet
a faded front page of the *Daily Star*
and you will read
ANGELS DROP PEACE PAMPHLETS ON BERLIN

Or a sudden flash of light
from a passing car, or the last flame from the sky
dying in agony, smoking and red,
may disclose the billboard silhouette
of a dumb Christ crucified.

Or the pavement will mock the echo of your feet,
a killer hidden in the dark
will pause to stare with lonely, hungry eyes
along the knife. . . .

43

POEM FOR ALL THE HEROES

There is blood on your hands
in your eyes
in your hair
on your lips.

There is the smell of children on you
smell of young girls
smell of old men
old women.

We can never forget this
nor forgive you

for one drop of innocent blood
dripping anywhere in the night.

THIS STREET OF THIS CITY

All those lost years
when our beach was a sidewalk
burning to the naked foot, our water molten tides
of asphalt leading to a distant shore,
our waves the crest of traffic—cars, trucks, buses—
the screaming of brakes our gulls crying. . . .

Too bad we've lost the ease of our childhood dreams—
they might be useful now in this street of this city,
where all the traffic in the world salutes our ears,
leaving only your beautiful body to cover
with the intense flowering braille of my evening thoughts.

44

ABSENCE

There are no lips to touch, melt into,
no hands running slowly through hair,
no body to wake beside, to feel
unbearably pressed to in the dark,
all five senses riotously reeling.

And so I curse this city,
hate to walk the sunlight streets
crowded with beautiful faces, superb bodies,
whose eyes looking into mine flash no greeting,
loathe warm-breathing mornings, passionate noons,

because from them all this image always rises up
to taunt, to torment me: you sighing gently
as your thighs brush mine
in that scalding meeting. . . .

45

THE GOING DOWN OF THE WIND

And so this wind
that struck our faces all day across these runways,
making us whine, run like stray dogs
before a boy with an upraised stone,

has died down now, blown out its strength,
its reckless young spirit, and like a colt newly broken,
stands panting now, ready for the saddle.

I like to think our hate will go this way,
our savage, unbridled hate, war madness,
love of killing, of mass destruction,

to think that the day of the crescendo
is fast approaching, that the flaming leaping
underground volcano of our world may even tomorrow
heave with the loudest lion's roaring man has yet heard,

that the blood-red lava of our meanest passions,
our deceit, our cancerous greed, our dreams of terror,
may plunge in savage streams across the earth,
then gradually brake their flow, and somehow, somewhere,
finally stop forever. . . .
                    So laugh if you like
at this fondest dream of mine,
but then you weren't with me in the wind today,
wind streaming like the aching touch of death
down these snow-savage runways. . . .

... and up there you lived closely together with eighty other airmen for nearly two months, came to know their meanness, fears, jealousy, lewdness, and above all the goodness in all of them, whether hidden deeply in their hearts or showing through every action. You felt the bond which the sight of another blue uniform on a dark street could give you, something which the others who didn't wear your colour knew nothing of, were the poorer for not knowing.

Strangely enough the things you worried about then were far different from all you'd considered so important in your life before—now it was pay parade, a booze-up, keeping your eyes open in class, leave, the new perfect prick of a flight-sergeant—you never talked about war news, strikes, politics, weekends at the cottage or getting the car for an evening of curb-cruising—for you the war news was no longer important, you couldn't strike or actively belong to a political party, and there was certainly no cottage, no car....

Instead there was the barrack corporal turning on the lights and yelling you out of bed at six of a winter's morning, breakfast at six-thirty and by seven-thirty the headlights of oncoming cars stunning your eyes with light as they flashed by you through the cold morning darkness, the sound of a hundred other pairs of boots hitting the roadway together the one sound that kept you warm and awake. Instead there was that last train of the good old London and Port Stanley Railway, with all seats taken and you standing between the cars watching the sleeping dark of the countryside rushing past you on either side, half-listening to a joke or story one of the boys might be telling, feeling tired and wanting to yawn (but you didn't want the others to know you were the least bit tired, so you held it back until you could let it out unnoticed), with finally the lights of St. Thomas up ahead, and the feeling that your journey for that day at least was nearly over, a little farther and you'd be home again....

When We Are Young
(1946)

GREEN, WONDERFUL THINGS

Those green temple-dancers of the trees
stretch their fresh, unspoiled arms
above the living forests of the grass.

Under a full-rounded moon
frogs blink back green-eyed moons.
Evenings I chose not to wrestle
with maidens there'll be still
the sinewy loins of my thoughts
to press open with the wonder
of a lanced star;

while still somewhere out there,
innocent yet menacing,
green, wonderful things
that often turn into enemies,
snapping blindfolds over lazy minds,
hiding all too easily
the sight and the smell of blood.

THE HUNTER

I carry the groundhog along by the tail
on the way back to the farm, the blood slowly dripping
from his mouth one or two drops at a time,
leaving a perfect trail for anyone to follow.

Your half-wit hired man
is blasting imaginary rabbits
far off to our left, while you and I move on
through fields steaming after rain,
jumping each mud patch.

As I walk I can't help noticing
the swing of your girl's hips ahead of me,
that and the proud way your hand
holds the shotgun.

And remembering how you held it
up to the limp hog caught in the trap
and blew his head off—
                    wonder now what fate
you may have in store for me.

51

APPLE-BLOW

1. HIM

I remember the orchards
stretching back row on row
from the oil-covered roads,
white, red and still,
with the blow heavy on them
weighing each branch down;
how we'd stand and watch a petal
shake itself loose in the wind,
then drift down so lightly, so easily,
to the blossom-strewn grass.

2. HER

I lie in the grass, apple blossoms
under me like a rug.
I roll my legs through the thick of them,
crushing their yielding softness, mad with the thoughts
that flash through my mind, dark, wonderful thoughts
of what he may do when he comes for me,
when his long legs climb the fence
and he kneels beside me, then takes me in his arms,
when I melt beneath his kiss
with his hands moving over my body,
soft, I hope, as these apple blossoms,
when his breath comes hot
with me lying under him in torment,
clutching white petals in my hand,
while the earth, the moon and the stars
rush together madly at each other. . . .

FOR SLEEPING

Now may the great bird Sleep
make a last homing sweep
above these houses.
                  Inhumanities, despair,
blotted out at the first closing circuit
of his flight.
            Then bid him settle
close by my love, and in my place,
touch a downy wing softly to her hair.

53

IS EVERYBODY HAPPY?

Doubt may exist, but evidence is everywhere at hand
to convince the most skeptical observer
of the kind efficiency of our civilization,
with nothing left to chance, everything provided
to make our stay on this earth a brief but happy interval.

For example, please enter the gates
of this modern mansion for the insane.
Observe the sweeping approaches, the simple but impressive
    architecture.
Come inside and walk the silent-tread corridors,
the miles of connecting tunnel. See how spotless everything is,
how skilfully the staff perform their duties.
Watch the happy faces of the patients all light up,
they thrive in this world of rest and sunshine.

(The bars on all the windows are unobtrusive.
The guards are efficient handlers.
The walls are well sound-proofed.
The patients are crazy anyway.)

Nothing's left to chance in our civilization, everything's
    provided,
and as further advances are made we can always build bigger,
    better, more efficient madhouses.

54

THE PENNY FLUTE

On the side street as we came along it in the darkness,
an old man, hat in front of him on the pavement,
was playing a penny flute.
                    The sound was small and sweet,
almost a whisper beside the heavy beat
of the cloth factory's machinery across the street,
(as if somehow he wasn't playing
for an audience at all, but only for himself).

We wondered who he was, and how long he'd been standing
piping that thin string of music.
                    But we were late for where
        we were going,
and young and impatient: we really didn't have time for old
        men and thin, lonely tunes,
especially tunes played on a penny flute. . . .

WHEN WE ARE YOUNG

The food was wonderful,
the whisky goes down smooth,
the radio has fifteen tubes.

But you sit over there,
I sit over here,
while the conversation eddies, ebbs,
with only the dance-bands
constant in their beat.

And we wait for that time
when it's proper and polite to leave,

because it's sheer agony
to sit apart, to talk,

when we are young
and have arms and have lips.

56

PHONY WAR

It seems that rifles fire blanks
or are cock-eyed as hell like the kind in shooting galleries,
while shells merely nudge you on the shoulder if you've
    overslept,
jangling your nerves a bit so you get sick leaves for nothing
    at all,
and flame-throwers are really pretty Roman candles
giving off crazy lighting especially after dark,
as for bayonets, we all know they come in handy
if the roast beef in the mess is a trifle rare....

O everyone has weekends off,
goes to bed with his lover or sometimes his wife,
with every last man a hero whose name will long be
    remembered
when the war is some day over:
                        and if you should accidentally
    die,
your soul will lie at peace on the breasts of a dozen angels.

57

THE LAGOON

My heart is that Hanlan's lagoon,
quiet, very still in its depths,
cool as the morning wind that rocks
the pads of the water-lily.

And you are that busy weed-cutter
steaming up-channel, long knives down-reaching
to my heart's deepest floor, then slashing hard
at my anchored-fast tranquillity.

Now look, the twisted tentacles
of my dreams, pushed to the surface,
float awhile, then are washed gradually ashore,
left to wither on the sand.

58

REVELATION

No doubt sometime later
(but not too much later)
sex will raise his ugly beautiful head.

Night will be coming down,
the neon of Joe's cutting streaks of blood
across the ceiling. Streets cold and dead,
full of unknown terror. Trees never looking more
like torn arms suspended
on wind-singing crosses.

All this at the window.
Then turning to discover
the peaceful lake of your flesh
before storm,
set down in the darkness
of a roomful of ghosts.

59

YOU LUCKY PEOPLE

It's really not too long to wait,
fifty, sixty years is only a breath of wind
in the face of Time (so *they* tell us).

Patience is the one great thing;
few have this virtue.

So don't forget—*you* are the lucky people,
even if we have estates in the country,
even if we blow a thousand on a weekend,
even if three limousines wait in the garage,
even if our fingers are tired cutting coupons;

honest to God it's you, not us,
truly with both hands on the bible we wish we were in your
     shoes,
you lucky people!

See the open envy on our faces as we look at you
sitting hollow-eyed, minds empty,
on dirty-littered stoops of smoke-blackened tenements
at the end of one-way streets.

AM

It's too soon to sleep after being with you,
my senses still burn, though the flame of you is gone,
and my eyes don't want to close yet
after seeing all they have seen,
while my hands, my lips, have stayed with you,
cupped at your breasts, drawn to your lips.

The word tomorrow sounds like eternity.

So with midnight long gone
I lie stretched on my bed, letting the late bands
on the radio ride through my mind,
until presently sleep shall come,
darkness blot you out by a subtle trick till morning.

HOME FRONT

So we watched pictures on a screen,
made islands of our brittle wit.

Afterward drove somewhere,
danced in the dark with the radio
beating, pulsing out gladness,
my senses lost in your hair.

Then in the car again
the dry wetness of your lips,
the long, cool wetness. . . .

While for all we knew
at that moment of moments,
he whom we both knew so well
could be lying somewhere
burnt crisp as a cinder,

or with chest ripped open,
was screaming for stretcher-bearers
who will never come.

62

WAITING

RCAF Station, Sydney, NS

Two nights of rain, three days of fog,
a dripping sound in the ears and the nuzzling gauze
unwound right to the barrack steps.

Monotony begins to prick its exquisite needle
into a widening circle of arms,
the eyes, lost to the touch of the sun,
turn deeper into their caves and eat the darkness.

The mind flickers, hangs balanced
on its delicate blue flame.

63

THE PATIENTS

Daily the sun increases on the southern windows,
flooding the antiseptic wards with gales of light
which strikes the long darkness of their eyes like scalpels
carving between the edge of rot and health,
loosening each thought of death their minds
held firm and fondled like a precious hope.

And these dwellers with pain, released on the southern porches,
see once again that world they knew only
as a dull, mindless roar heard through stone-lipped walls,
feel trees just beyond unfolding their umbrellas
of glistening green, heard bird-song brave above traffic,
almost laugh again to see children darting on the sidewalks,

and with their hearts beating so they could almost weep,
stare upward, watch with their souls almost lost in the sky,
the swoop and climb of a lone airplane.

64

YOUNG GIRLS

With night full of spring and stars we stand
here in this dark doorway and watch the young
girls pass, two, three together, hand in hand.
They are like flowers whose fragrance hasn't sprung
or awakened, whose bodies now dimly feel
the flooding, upward welling of the trees;
whose senses, caressed by the wind's soft fingers, reel
with a mild delirium that makes them ill at ease.

They lie awake at night, unable to sleep,
then walk the streets, kindled by strange desires;
they steal lightning glances at us, unable to keep
control upon those subterranean fires.
We whistle after them, then laugh, for they
stiffen, not knowing what to do or say.

65

THE UNMISTAKABLE SWEETNESS

The unmistakable
sweetness of you
spills over me like wine.

So don't seem surprised
if I grin and laugh
at nothing at all.

It's much the same way
a man out of prison must feel
with his first free look at the sky,

or a young colt turned loose
into a field, his thin legs
shivering with sheer delight.

66

THE ROOM ON PRINCE STREET

Yes, the room is liveable, with the heater on it is almost warm, while the postcards of the Union Station, of the harbour, of Bay Street looking north to the City Hall, but even more so the double-paged, coloured, seductive pose of Rita Hayworth from this month's *Esquire*, relieve the walls of much of that fatal, familiar bareness, that emptiness always present in varying, overpowering degrees.

And yes, the bed is comfortable, and sleep mostly comes easily, except for those really cold nights when you know there's no use getting up for extra blankets, as only a certain body there close beside you would have any chance of covering you in soft, warm-breathing sleep.

And of course there's plenty of space for your books, those well written gateways of escape, and the piles of magazines from *New Masses* to *Down Beat*, all full of tricky, easy talk.

And let's not forget the radio, the late-night bands served up direct from Manhattan's ballrooms, the news of the world rattled off in five fast minutes of censored, half-lying communiqués (but all of it better than that long, long unending silence broken only by the roar of an exhaust shaking the night outside the window!)

That window facing out on the street, the street where the young girls sweep along on their wonderful legs, where the old and the cripples hobble by, where soldiers pass grinding the cleats of their boots into the roadway.

And lastly the door of this room that leads to the stairs to the street to a world going slowly mad, but not really knowing or caring why.

THE BARRACKS

How beautiful the sleepers!

Innocence has clamped the obscure mouths,
sealed the boy-lewd minds,
touched the sad, the mocking tender eyes.

The lights have been out an hour.
The only noises water running somewhere,
a muffled voice, engines revving up in nearby hangars.

The silence here is so like death,
while the innocent, sleeping faces
wouldn't look out of place framed with white lilies,
tapped of blood, each a chilled marble.

68

THE EVENING HOUR

Sitting at the table with friends and a couple of beers,
night outside, quiet and bright in here,
relaxing after work, talking of this and that—
the pennant race, that new girl at the office,
a striptease at the last stag party—

while over there, far across the winter Atlantic,
terror stalks through the streets, monotony grinds in the
    shelters,
bombers web their way across the city, bombs whistle and sleek
    noses dig
into the entrails of slums, docks, mansions,
catch the innocent in their homes, then vanish in the night
as the flames light up the dead, questioning faces of children. . . .

Yes, the beer certainly tastes flat,
the hour seems late, and we are suddenly tired, very tired,
of the office, of all the girls, of all the stories, of all the times
bright, gay, crude, sad or merely dull,
of waking, sleeping, thinking, hating, fearing, wondering,
    hoping,

a little tired of life,
a little ashamed of warm blood bought so easily, so cheaply,
by a world of monsters,
haunted, we now admit, by the glassy, ghostly look
of unknown, countless eyes that stare and stare at us,
bewildered, accusing.

69

POSTSCRIPT

*They wrote in the old days that it is sweet and fitting to die
for one's country. But in modern war there is nothing sweet
nor fitting in your dying. You will die like a dog for no good
reason—Ernest Hemingway.*

Trouble is you won't even die like a dog.
Most of the dogs I've noticed died fast and clean,
their guts on the road or pavement in a neat little pile. . . .

Instead you'll die very slowly, having oceans of time
to think about it all, O plenty of time
before you finally can't spit out enough blood
building up in your mouth, and you choke on it,
(but always remember it was your own red blood
and a colourful way to kick the bucket). . . .

But the biggest problem still with this running of a war
is the plain simple fact that the worms haven't learned their
    place,
didn't have their radios on when the pot-belly government
    boys
were shooting off their certified crap to the whole wide
    world—
their sweet, touching low-down on life, liberty and the
    pursuit of virgins—

So the poor little crawlers don't know anything more
than that they feel mighty hungry, so anything they see
they eat because they can't bear starving to death, or so it
    seems:

and all those dead bodies lying out there going nowhere fast
look mighty good to the little devils, so out they come crawling
on their bellies in open order
and get busy quick-like. . . .

Too bad they're not humans,
they'd know better for sure.

ERSATZ

Kiss her now, kiss her a thousand times,
over and over rub your cheek to hers, feel it burn you,
    scorching as the touch of flame,
finger her breasts almost savagely, until they seem to grow
    huge in your hands.

Then for a moment body to body strangely still,
eyes through the darkness watching the snow's ghostly gleam
under the streetlight there beyond the window,
wonder why it's not the same, why it's no good, no good any
    more,
no good at all, and how long, you, can you go on fooling
    yourself about the others,

how long before the emptiness will go, or will it always
keep aching and crying and killing somewhere in the darkness.

71

Other Canadians
(1947)

QUEEN STREET SERENADE

What bantamweight champ is training this week at the Apex,
what fair young thing (under grease-paint) will knock 'em
   dead at the Casino
with belly-roll to traps:
              who works the old beats,
who drinks the most at all the hotels, who has the latest dose,
best soft touch, surest tips, most advanced set of bug-eaten
   lungs,

with the dirt, dust, heat, cheapness, easy virtue, hidden fear,
   screams, crazy laughs,
still on both sides of the coin
no matter what month, what day, what hour you flip it,

both sides of the coin
what day what hour what tick of what clock.

74

AFTER DARK

Perhaps because I've also had so much of my loving
in the shadows of nighttime parks, on the cold-lipped sands
    of beaches,
anywhere two bodies could lie, be close together,
so hands could reach out to feel the fond, desired flesh,
O anywhere under sweep of trees, with the smell of grasses,
that each could know earth's nearness, mute sympathy,
sense her wind-whispered blessing, and not be afraid
of the peeping-tom public eye, with all the polared thoughts
of its steadily shrivelling inch of mind, never easily measured—

Perhaps because of all of this
I feel a firm kinship, like brother to sister,
for these young bodies sprawled out here tonight
in the lie of their loving: know the leg-curled tightness, the
    soft roundness of them,
the sweet torture that transforms them, that pushes them high
    above
drab work at the office, banal situations, all the long, empty
    hours of their lives—

and walk past them quietly, a little wistfully, looking straight
    ahead,
each echo of my footsteps seeming to sound out *alone, alone....*

DEFINITIONS

"Cities are butcher shops, love is confusion, war is a flame-thrower, our young men are bandaged"—letter from David Mullen, 6 September, 1946.

Cities are butcher shops. . . .
Of course you've seen the way
the meat is displayed
on the principal thoroughfares—
young girls plump chickens,
older hags tough rump roast,
and everyone has a price,
some written right on their faces,
others stamped lightly on buttocks
well hidden under lightweight girdles;
while God the Almighty Butcher
leans above the counters of skyscrapers,
spitting now and again
on the sawdust floor of the streets.

Love is confusion. . . .
Love is also death
to so many easy victims,
the hastily thrown-off dress,
the sticky condom,
love is a stairway leading down from heaven,
love is poverty endured,
face turned to the other fangs
of the world's open hatred,
love is everywhere and of all time,
love is a being together when apart.

War is a flame-thrower....
Tell me, what must it feel like
to sneak through the woods till you get a bead
on the fanciest pillbox you've ever seen,
turn the juice on full, then watch the flames
pour through the gun-slits as you hear
somebody give a cry like a little kid
at about the same time you begin to smell
the stench of burning bodies—tell me, Mr. Flame-Thrower,
was it as much fun as that girl you took last night?

Our young men are bandaged....
Our young men are also lost,
but they curse to themselves and go on stumbling,
striking faces against the multiplying walls;
our young men will never cry out,
they bite back the pain, somehow swallow the anguish
like a green bile surging up in the mouth;

O our young men are the comrades
we must always walk beside,
we must understand and pity,
but above all understand.
Their voices will be the poet in us speaking,
and if we should be great it is only because of them.

Go to Sleep, World
(1947)

KITE IN THE WIND

Young boy with your kite
high up and sailing with the wind,
a huge bird now diving, twisting as the breeze
toys and frolics with it, driving it higher, higher
toward the sun one moment, then as suddenly
pitching it, plunging it earthward,
so close to scraping, lancing the trees,
before that wind laughs,
drives it sleek and skyward again:

watch closely this vibrant, coloured snake
trapped on the end of your wrist,
which you fly these untroubled afternoons
in the golden morning of your life.

Some day when you're much older you'll remember
such a kite in the wind—as you recall that life
since toyed with, dashed about by the world—

first it was that rocket ride
shooting toward the stars on passion, huge happiness,
then despair's sudden, bottomless air-pocket,
failure's almost heart-stopping stall,
the dark dive through earth's blackest hours....

Some day, yes, you may remember this,
but today, thank God, there's only the wind,
the sun high and far above the leaves,
your kite at the end of its cord
twisting, leaping through the playtime air!

WHEN NIGHT COMES

Not in the noonday crowds,
not at waking,
not with the warm, hard sunlight
in the park, on office windows:

no, it's certainly not then,
rather it's when the sun has gone, when lights shine in the
    streets,
when people go home through those streets, couples closely
    together,
it begins with the switch pulled on day, the throwing-on of
    night.

Do you ever feel it? Do you ever want to cry just a little,
but you find that the tears won't come?
Do you ever feel an emptiness, do you ever reach out somehow
    in the dark
for warmth, for understanding—but clutch only empty
    fingers?

Like tonight, with the madness starting, slowly building,
with her absent somewhere miles across town, as if it were
    forever,
with me here alone with a strange, new, terrible loneliness,
me here in this night all darkness, clocks, silences.

ALL THE THRONES OF THEIR KINGDOMS

I haven't yet found the right words,
though Lord only knows I've tried
to tell you what you mean to me,
what my poor life would be without you.

So all I can do is kiss you
until you moan, wrap my arms
around all your loveliness, hold you hard
until these arms ache.
                       And though I know
you understand, it's still not enough,
not nearly enough, as I sit down
again and again at my desk, only half-alive
from my love of you, put down words,
many words on this paper before me,

but it's still not enough,
there simply are no words to fit you,
nothing on earth to compare to you:

O all the thrones of their kingdoms
shake as you walk outside their cowering walls!

SUNDAY NIGHT WALK

Sunday night we go to church,
and after the benediction when the doors swing open
into our world of human joy and weakness,

we slowly walk along the avenue,
finding ourselves among crowds very restless and alive,
although there is nothing for anyone to do
but walk and re-walk this street, jam the corner restaurants.

Then suddenly we're away again
from the noise of autos, streetcars,
even the glare of streetlights, now aware for the very first time
of stars high above us—and so close they seem to brush
    our heads—
the gently traced-in silhouettes of trees.

And look, this is grass, fresh-smelling greenness,
the pond at the bottom of the hill a real pond,
with a real moon riding it,
even the two ducks floating on it are real.
So it seems too that we are real, our love is real,
the world around us real, very real.
But admit it, the world, like us,
is tired, very tired of reality,
seeks to hide from it every chance it gets,

even as we ourselves now hide in the shadows.

CASA LOMA

The guide reviews the high spots of the tour—
the copper doorway worth ten thousand dollars,
the secret staircase and the master bedroom,
the great hall and the endless endless cellars—

and out we come into the wind and sunshine,
now hurrying to leave it far behind—
this hideous waste, this monument to money,
so clear in meaning even to the blind!

ST. JOHN WOMAN

You've never belonged here,
this was never really meant to be,
here where there's only death and the smell of death
in these ageing houses, rotted wharves,
along these cracked, madly sloping pavements
well mixed with fog and rain,
grey fog and endless rain. . . .

No, you've never belonged here,
you are much too beautiful,
too shining-clear of mind
not to have escaped this,
you who should be fêted, loved madly
in a dozen cities,

while here you are wasted, truly wasted,
you who light up this fine room tonight
with a brilliance not of this city by the sea.

THE FALLING OF THE SNOW

The falling of the snow—
white rice of a marriage of joy
thrown softly, sifted silently down
from the church steps of heaven.

Look up, taste its whiteness,
breathe its stainless purity,

falling all without favour
on the head of the magnate
and the bum with his head in the garbage,

draping the graves of our young, late, foolish dead,
and the strangely silent killer's lips of the guns.

RAINY EVENING DOWNTOWN

The rain that will not turn to snow,
the evening darkness darkening,
the crowds that slowly thicken now
up Bay, on Richmond, along King.

The dripping face of the newsboy,
the warm lights shining from hotels,
the slender figures raincoat-dry,
and out of restaurants the smells.

The sparkling entrances to shows,
the pavements that recall the black
and savage testaments of those
who passed but never will come back.

THE HATED CITY

We will go, you and I,
to the hated city.

Come in from the lake
over green-blue water,
slip between white beaches
and islands of willow,
see the morning sun
proudly striking her battlements.

We will lunch at the Savarin,
a little later sip wine
at a place no-one knows,
much later slowly stroll
under chestnut trees in blossom,
finally ride to our room
ten magic floors skyward,
with midnight long gone
and only the faint click
of lovers' heels over pavement
as we take our last look
at golden lights, shining lights
strung out everywhere
in twinkling fairy rows. . . .

We will go, you and I,
to the hated city.

A WIND

A wind sweeps through the grass
like a woman's hair with the fingers of her lover
running through it in the high-keyed moments of love,
twists savagely the branches of trees
till they toss like the lost masts of shipwrecks.

A month ago my love was like this wind,
sweeping through my head with all this same madness same
      strength,
and nothing could stand before it, nothing!
All doubts, fears, O everything
faded like smoke: I walked, a young god
at the beginning of a world.

MORNING

Sometime near morning I awake.

The clock ticks away on the dresser,
a light wind is nagging the blind,
no noise yet from the street.

The sound of your breathing
is the only living sound,
the rise and fall of your breasts
morning's first wonder.

You are so beautiful this way—
why must I ever awaken you?

LOWER YONGE STREET

Looking down Yonge Street see the flashing neon,
the red, green banners of the city's magic,
trick deceivers of the unwary, wooing, calling you
down into the winking canyons:

                              to learn all too soon
that the lights up close are cold, mechanical,
the restaurants cheerless, bars empty of all but a pleasing
    darkness,
crowds on the pavements aimless, restless, as truly bewildered
    as you will ever be,
even with all that flashing neon,
those darting red-green banners.

NORTH OF TORONTO

Whatever else in this great year of death,
worms in the brain and bloated belly,
whatever else is doomed to mix with dust
or rot like stinking Europe—
                    this land, these fields,
the red barns, standing cattle, lazy villages
north of Toronto stretching to Georgian Bay and the sterner
    land
of a thousand lakes, short birch and mossed boulder—
all this is permanent, will be here long after I'm gone
and the unborn generations likewise gone....

Here the city changes, they tear down the house
around the corner, cut out a new street, block up an old one,
and soon attack each precious landmark, those haunts
tangled up so wonderfully with memories; suddenly it seems
they're gone, and they've left us nothing, nothing....

But this great stretch of Ontario
will remain to be looked at in two years or two hundred,
the same rich beauty flashing by the desperate bus,
same balm of peace, of quiet living,
in all the sleepy towns, the slumbering villages.

JUNE, 1945

RCAF Station, Croft, Durham

There, O there,
see how suspended, how like gulls
of some fabulous age,
                              side-slipping,
veering, O prancing like colts
let off the rope, whole fields
for them to romp in,
kings for a day
in their mane-shaking, careless young strength—

this last trio of bombers going home,
quitting this England they've come to know
intimately, with a giant love,
and leaving behind a red trail across Europe,
where their anger finally spit fire, drew blood
in the last agony of its death,
(death running like a thousand rivers,
with these the angry leeches
on a rotten, long-corrupt flesh).

Bright flares shower above them, around them,
all the gayest colours on this too-grey day
not enough to show that all the hearts left here
now swoop with them, dive with their every boyish pass
over these fields, these runways, silent now—

and O God, please forever. . . .

BOURNEMOUTH

Bournemouth offers, in rising tiers from the water below to up,
    up somewhere at the level of the trees,
a mass of luxury hotels—browns, greys, reds, mustard yellows
    —all ugly protruding, which would geometrically please
the eye of an idiot; offers stores, gardens, terminals and squares
where the best people can escape from the smoke, the drab of
    northern cities, can throw away their cares

and against the falls and winters of their lives begin the
    foundations, outer bastions of their pitiful defence
against the panzers of death grinding closer—buying time
    with their miserable pounds, shillings, pence.

SOLDIERS, 1945

Will they be changed when they come back?

Will all the years of loneliness,
of learning to be men,
give them the strength they'll need in this new world?

Will the years of danger sharpen them
to the hidden dangers—letting them read beneath
hollow words, empty acts?
Will the years of death make them prouder,
more sure of life, from meeting that grim one
face to face? Will the years of leanness
sicken them to the plenty
of the corrupt few, sharpen the necessary hatred?
And will those years of hate
ripen to a new love, fuller understanding?

Or will those years teach them nothing,
so they come back innocent as children
to the eager arms of exploiters,
to the bondage of their grasping loves?

Come back to greater seasons of rot,
fresh advances of death,
the ruins of a truly dying world?

DUROCHER STREET

If when I come the next time
up this evening-quiet street, walking slowly
past the old-fashioned fronts of apartment houses,
each one with the same silent grace
the streets of Paris must have; children playing
their before-bedtime games, neighbours talking
doorstep to doorstep, trees tossing
their summer-green capes through the slow dusk,
sounds of traffic far away, almost stilled now;

if when I come the next time
down the sidewalk level with your apartment,
and looking up, should see your face there,
framed in the open window,
staring perhaps out into early darkness—
that expressionless face of yours which expresses everything
in its firm nobility, its deep-searching eyes—

then right away I'd make this street akin to heaven,
would call on God to bless its every house,
would pray for two angels to watch always at your door,
the sun to shine gold forever on these pavements.

LISTENING TO THE RAIN

It would be nice tonight to lie beside you
on your closed-in verandah, close together
on the same soft comfort of the couch
we know from last summer, listening again
to the small, nervous feet of the rain at first faltering,
then sprinting hard across the shingles,
its noise in the downspouts the rude gurgling sound
of a thirsty man upping a bucket
of cold water down his throat, at the same time overflowing
face, chest, arms in one chilled outpouring. . . .

But mostly there's something sleepy-peaceful about rain,
something of love in it, a dreamy falling
through the spaces of heaven to the earth—
even war waits for rain to go
as if afraid to enter its sanctuary.

So it would be nice tonight with you and the rain,
then every now and then the rain gone from our thoughts,
to come back so suddenly drumming in our silly ears
it almost would match the hunted beating of our hearts.

94

THIS POEM WILL NEVER BE FINISHED

This poem will never be finished,
will be written over and over
this year, next year, every year.

This poem is you,
this poem is your face,
your hair, your hands,
O all of you,

and I am your poet
who will always be singing
more beautiful songs as you stand
in splendour beside the eternal rose.

IN LOVE

I'm sick with my love for you,
go around all day
not caring what I see or do
between these hours
of being away from you.

O all their cleverness
their fine talk
their brightest theories,
fade like some insubstantial mist
before your all-embracing sun.

My love the most wonderful disease
a man could wish to die of.

SHEDIAC BLUES

The little cottages are all asleep,
the last bus with its passengers is gone,
the ocean licks in slowly over the flats,
and the present is drawn

much like these shutters, while the past invades
the all-too-silent silence of this room,
with the warm night at the window just the night,
the bed without you colder than the tomb.

PUPPETS

It was all so Bohemian,
so light-hearted, gay,
everyone seemed to have a wonderful time
on absolutely nothing,
which in itself would have been unique
except that inevitably you knew
someone at sometime would have to foot the bill—
tomorrow even, or next week or next year.

And it was all pitched on so high a key
you wondered what sure voice would break first,
which effortlessly laughing face
would burst suddenly into tears,
and everyone so pulsing, so alive,
you wondered when the ambulance would arrive,
whose cold body would be found on the bedroom floor.

APART

What was missing all last night
was the plain simple fact of your presence,
and over all the smart talk,
above all the bored talk,
I prayed for a word from you that never came.

Or to put it another way:
in some hours of time and place that were all dead,
there was a crying out for the living heart of you.

97

THE UNBREAKABLE

So we've come together again
as easily it seems as a gull's wing
dips above water, touches it,
then rising flicks a single drop away.

If we've changed any
it's to have grown a little wiser;
but then, the world has also changed,
and most of us in it,
having grown more brutal perhaps,
having lost much of our simple tenderness.

Sometimes I feel I don't know
my own people anymore,
or even wish to know them. . . .

But you and I, we're much the same,
nothing really has changed between us;
the world may scar us, may break us,
but it can never hunt out, much less destroy
what we've both hidden in our secret hearts.

GONE

Like some receding face or form in the fog
you go from me, and I know
that all the lifting of the grey veils will not show
your dazzling sun lighting my morning world.

LOVERS, DOMINION SQUARE

They more than anyone else
wouldn't understand my haste
in getting in out of the rain,
in leaving this wind-whipping night
for the tavern's warm heart—all its steaming food,
sparkling wine, and the music of the violin.

They seem as much a part of the rain
as the policeman on the corner with the white cape
and white rubber boots to the thighs,
standing in the streaming traffic's centre
and directing with an effortless hand.

They seem almost part of the night, these two lovers,
with their slow, lingering steps, their total unawareness
of everything in this city but their love,
the strength, the honest lust in their bodies touching
as they walk across the square. . . .

99

RESERVE

There will be another night,
there will be another day,
there will be bright tomorrows
blurring by in bewildering succession
like boxcars of a fast freight
flashing their level-crossing nightmare.

There will be others to love,
others to betray,
with always new faces,
always untouched delights,
for certain new tortures, new desires,

and as if all this
weren't simply enough,
a fresh approach to death.

ON A DOCK IN ST. JOHN

The day was windy, with not too much sun,
that time we stood on a dock in St. John
with the wind whipping through our airmen's blues,
and watched a dingy freighter going through
the slow routine of clearing port.

A gang of boys, roughly our age,
leaned on her rails, dirty-clothed, loud talkers,
and as the ship's hull drifted clear
of the dock they waved at us,
yelled something in a language we didn't understand.

Did they envy us? Did they wish
they were in the uniform of their country?
We doubted that very much.

But at that moment
we certainly envied them.
They were careless, and free,
and most of all
they were going somewhere.

FALLING OF THE ACORNS

Close together as one,
ears, eyes as one,
lying here in the matted sunshine
slipping down through the trees,
sliding down to the grass
with its litter of leaves,
golds, browns, yellows, crimsons.

Both of us nearly motionless
through the long voyage of the afternoon,
no word spoken, hardly a sound made between us,
everything said with a touch of fingers, press of lips,
so we hardly noticed the crashing partridge
who came on us suddenly in his blundering.

Bodies together as one,
ears, eyes as one,
listening with a patience born of long silence
for the deliberate, long-spaced falling of the acorns.

PORTRAIT OF ELINOR

The music could be sweet or low-down barrel-house,
that doesn't matter; neither does this room
in three-quarter darkness, and equally the beer
in tall, slender glasses at our elbow
is nice, but not important.

But her lithe, small body, quick hands on hips,
the agitated, shocky red hair, sure, swift tongue—
O these are minor wonders to outlive this year,
even you and I in this colourless time—

And oh yes, the small growl of our poetry.

SECOND MEETING

We sat in the little park,
and the lights from the cars going up the road
raised and lowered like a blind
bright magic across your face,
while your eyes held a shine like phosphorus,
your lips seemed the entrances to ruby caves.

We could see our breath easily in the dark,
but we were warm, the night was warm,
and I was drunk on the new wine of knowing you.

It seemed funny, though: here was I
aching to get away from this graveyard city,
then yesterday I'd met you,
and already you were throwing sand
into the well-oiled machinery of my plans.

TOGETHER AGAIN

Today I don't give a damn
about anything, anybody. The whole crooked, crawling world
can writhe and wriggle in its slime
without a blink from either eyelash.

All I want is the sun
going through me with its healing,
just the glimpse of a bird or a flower.

Please add to this, of course,
the magic thought to fondle and re-fondle
that all my long century of winter darkness
is over now, even gone forever,
because we're together again.

NEED OF AN ANGEL

Bushes lean in the wind,
feeling it soft now,
feeling the hand of spring
cupped at their breasts,
shaking their limbs
with sudden ice, then fire;
buds stir, throw their green
murmurous world above the dirt.

In me spring wakens,
wind catches my hair,
eyes ache in the sun
with the diamond-cut brilliance.

But who will come to touch me into fire,
who push the hesitant saplings into light,
who start an eddy through this stagnant heart,
who lead through forests of darkness to the dawn?

SUNNYSIDE AMUSEMENT PARK

Dark tunnel of love, the snaking roller-coaster
leaving a long trail of shrieks shaking up the darkness,
raw impact of faces, bodies, surging around corners,
red lips, silk legs, cowboy hats, uniforms,
with laughter or boredom tightly drawn
on bleached or rosy mask:
                          with always the feeling
of night crouched beyond this blaze of lights
and in it stars and a moon: but none of these
of this barker's hoopla world, this loud restlessness,
at one with our great lake at the beach's end
stretching cool, stretching far into a saner night.

HAPPY NEW YEAR

We stood in the middle of the dance-floor,
both of us with one eye on the clock,
the other on the bulging rainbow clusters
of balloons high above us waiting midnight.

Then when the horns began shrieking,
when the crazy people started shouting,
and we kissed in the middle of that bedlam,

there were suddenly only two in our world,
the balloons floated down, bounced unnoticed,
about our unheeding heads.

NIGHT WATCH

Not at Angelo's with wine and spaghetti,
not at the Oak Room, or Joe's, Mabel's or Tim's Place,
enclosed by no four walls, circled by no idle chatter,
not firmly held by the unseen hands of music,

but here with the lean cold pushing all light from the stars,
here under ghost buidings with silence grown too silent,

you and I in this doorway
kissing the night with bitter cigarettes.

107

GIRL ASLEEP

Leaving the amusement park behind,
the high weaving clarinet
from the too-crowded dance floor
mixed with the faraway roar
of the roller-coaster, clang-clang of shooting-galleries—

to drive down the river road, our headlights
picking out the stillness of hanging branches
in the warm summer night; then catching sudden gleams
off the water of the river just below,
while the house-lights on the cliffs above
lean through the darkness to join with the bonfires of
    corn-roasts,
red flames licking hard at the dark riding-cloak of night.

You are asleep now on my shoulder
in the back seat of the car,
and sleep seems to give your face
a beauty, a classic dignity,
which I'm afraid will be lost
at the first moment of your waking.

Sometimes I think death could make a queen of you,
but then I'd sooner have you ugly and alive—
the world has need of those who can truly live.

SHAKE HANDS WITH THE HANGMAN

From Casa Loma looking down
the city—
shower of lights at a roadside carnival.

It's cold now in the streets,
winter's coming.
His white whip waits
to be swung with a crack
in our stupid, grinning faces.

The man selling flowers outside Child's
has the nervous, shifting eyes of the hunted.

Shake hands with the hangman.
Notice how steady those hands are
after such bloody work.

Shower of lights . . .
white whip of winter . . .
eyes of the hunted . . .

Notice how steady those hands are
thick with the blood of this city.

109

YONGE STREET SATURDAY NIGHT

Except when the theatre crowds engulf the sidewalks
at nine, at eleven-thirty,
this street is lonely, and a thousand lights
in a thousand store windows
wouldn't break her lips into a smile.

There are a few bums out,
there are lovers with hands held tightly,
there are also the drunk ones
but they are princes among men, and are few.

And there are some like us,
just walking, making both feet move out ahead of us,
a little bored, a little lost, a little angry,

walking as though we were honestly going somewhere,
walking as if there was really something to see
at Adelaide or maybe on King,
something, no matter how little
that will give us some fair return
on our use of shoe-leather,

something perhaps that will make us smile
with a strange new happiness,
a lost but recovered joy.

OUR NIGHT

Night-time will return again, there'll be
the drinking sound of rain through the trees,
other feet will walk
on the sodden, thick-strewn death of the leaves,
and other arms will link together, other voices talk closely
    of this or that,
their shadows seized, then tossed by the light of every street-
    lamp. . . .

But our night will never be the same night again,
rain falling heavier or lighter, with a different murmur
    through the trees,
those leaves blown by the wind never cluttering the sidewalks
    quite the same,
arms of the walkers held much farther apart,
voices higher, their chattering even more senseless than our
    own,

all shadows grotesque, unreal,
intruding on our own that pass and re-pass
to the slow tempo of our ghostly footsteps.

т т т

NOCTURNAL

Sweep the birds down in their trees,
stop the merry-go-round, the sugar-candy mixer,
relax arm, leg and head, let the night drop its curtain
down the street where the moths hive about the street-lights,
let the wind blow, sing, steal into, circle round,
and let us pretend

for a minute, an hour, for several hours,
that hate, anger and violence,
hunger and pain, hiding and revenge
are gone forever.

THE NEST

It will have to be near water
so there can be moonlight like a pool
to bathe our tired, sleep-heavy eyes.

There must be a high, strong roof
so the rain children will not break
the step of their marching above us.

Needing of course the softest white sheets
to lull our tired flesh asleep
after we've squeezed all the love we can from our bodies,

with God's presence at the door
so none can touch the slightest scattered hair
of your head on its pillow,
that none will hand me a gun again and say,
leave her, there's more young blood to be spilled
in the name of our latest lie.

ON THE BROWN BED OF OUR CHOOSING

On the brown bed of our choosing
she lies beside me clothed in softest slumber.

A deer at rest in some sleepy woodland
couldn't lie with more easily flowing grace.

O her beauty is open to all the world
for the more fortunate to look upon,

while I lie awake beside her,
hearing the nervous-thudding rain
pacing the roof, and over it the winds
of the autumn, cold and desolate season.

Now something starts to cry inside of me—
perhaps the fears of past loneliness,
perhaps the thought of the coming iron winter,
the blankness of snow-hung mornings;

and I know I must risk waking her,
to be closer to that warm, breathing body,
to be closer to the source of that light
shining down on the calm castle of our love.

IT IS BECOMING GREY NOW

It is becoming grey now
the sun gone

It is becoming dark now
with light of day gone

It is becoming neither
night nor day now

It is becoming nothing
nothing nothing now

and everything gone.

DREAMS WERE ALWAYS CHEAP

Goodnight, darling, go to sleep now,
close your eyes and dream and dream and dream.
Dreams were always cheap—they're just as cheap now—
with the bad ones always better than they seem.

I also have my dreams, but they're too tender
to risk being maimed and broken by this time:
lean nervous years when the password is surrender,
and a poem is a poem because it has a rhyme.

YORKSHIRE VILLAGE

The world goes by this village, all villages like these,
wars and nightmares of wars, they drift by like clouds above
    the trees
that shield the cottages; life is just as it has been
for centuries—same equal proportion of love and laughter,
    striving and sin—

and this beer that we drink now, freshly tapped from the
    barrels on the landing below
to the landlord's huge pitcher to our glass is but part of the slow
round of centuries of habit and enjoyment, the game of the
    dart-players by dim candle-light
in the miniature inn-room the same game their fathers,
    grandfathers played.

And as our trucks finally pull away we've only one prayer
    tonight—
may the people here please forgive all the noise the wild
    Canadians have made.

116

THESE WORDS, THIS MUSIC

Although we've been singing now for more than an hour
it's only as the darkness builds, as stars pierce through,
that the music of the two accordions, the words of our mouths,
raised in these thousand-throated songs, take on beauty,

a pathos never intended, something we never dreamed
could or would ever happen. So we sing on and on,
not wanting to end this warmth, this comradeship
flowing suddenly like good wine, a feeling electric
flashing invisible sparks along the whole crowded deck length:
while this good ship speeding us home from Europe's madness,
    pulses, shivers,
as its funnels lay plumes on the wake of seething water.

These words we sing, this music playing,
our heartfelt thanks rising up to the heavenly angels.

117

TREES AFTER RAIN

Trees after rain
lean against the wind
clean-limbed, wet,
every inch delicate

as young girls coming from a pool
to stand naked in the sun,
water dripping from their flanks,
their shy, awakening breasts.

POEM FOR A SNAPSHOT

Behind you the lake, the boat, the sand,
but I really can't see past your body
draped in its windblown covering,
cannot see past your smile,
your upturned hair.

You need no backgrounds,
no-one would notice them anyway.

O my warm goddess,
slip down from this wall
and we'll span the darkness
of two years' parting
in our eyes' and our lips'
first touching together.

FRIDAY NIGHT

The waves come in with the same little fits and starts,
moths hive the same yellow lamps on the same sleepy streets,
the same Ward's Island lights march their glow-points on and
    on
into a darkness swallowing sky and water, into the peace
and coolness of the lake on a hot summer evening.

This is where we lay on the sand, my arm cradling your head,
this is where we talked of, whispered many things, some very
    foolish, all very real,
this is where we kissed, this is where night lengthened
with no thought of time or place or anything at all.

Are there more nights when we'll shape this sand to our bodies,
are there more words to mouth carelessly like pennies,
some to handle carefully as kittens,
will our lips still touch in the same, warm-charged welcome,
will all the clocks cease chiming,

with only the stars and their jewel-bright sparkle
in the backdrop of the sky, and a few far lights
on the water to salute us?

PRINT OF THE SANDPIPER

The three-pronged print the sandpiper has traced
into this sand before we came along,
is as firm, as definite a mark
as any of us can hope to leave
on the broad sand beach of our world.

In an hour the tide will come flooding in,
and after it's gone the sand will be unmarked
and fresh again, only the sea's touch on it,

even the print of the sandpiper
smoothed away by that effortless hand.

120

City Hall Street
(1951)

THE HIGHWAY

Take, take this four-laned highway complete with tricky
    cloverleafs,
speed up to sixty, seventy, eighty, slowing down to thirty idling
    through the main streets of sleepy towns
where the natives gawk, the children scream: on, on, on,
go like an eagle swooping through a valley—trees, barns,
    fenceposts one unending blur:
then run her up on a smooth stretch—eighty, ninety, a
    hundred—hold her there,
heart beating much faster now, mind registering this lyric
    thought:
we are only beginning to live now, the tempo is becoming
plainer—
ears singing with the humming motor as the sportscar with
    all the latest features
leaps ahead to where and for what and to hell with it anyway.

WHEN I SEE OLD MEN

When I see old men
with their noses in books
every night in dead corners
of deserted rooms;

when I notice the look
they give young girls
passing by in the street
that ends with a sigh;

when I hear the petty boasting
a glass of beer lights in them,
the inevitable memories
of their once near-greatness;

then I pray my old age
shall be just as brief
as the fluke matador's
one golden season—

year unmarked by horns,
overflowing with contracts,
and cries that re-echo
round the hoarse arena.

A DREAM OF HANLAN'S

(Southern England, 1945)

It's not homesickness, it's the thought of the morning sun
strong on the beach, warming the sand for the feet
of the young girl and boy I can almost see running
out the cottage door, down the walk, then free of the house
and anything holding them from the lake's tingling-cool
    water. . . .

And it isn't loneliness, it's just me imagining
the utter peace of mind, the quiet of those mornings,
when no aircraft roared off to bomb or to destroy,
no machine-guns, no cannon, shaking out sprays of death,
but with only the shouts of swimmers in the water,
the cries of the children as the waves break on their impractical
castles of sand.
               It's nothing but desire to live again,
fresh from the beginning like a child.

BAR, HARLEM

Dark faces that drift in from avenues
ghostly with light and heavy with the death
of another day somehow endured, now forgotten.
Faces without emotion, each crouched on their stool,
bourbon and chaser before them on the gleaming bar-top,
dark, restless hands on their glasses. And more faces lost
in a group of laughter, deep-throated, crude,
eyes gleaming, pulsating bodies alive
out on the barroom floor, lithe bodies
under long coats, acting their lives out
in pantomime:
                    each one a king
of a great kingdom, shining and far away,
where there's no darkness of city or of mind.

SPEAKERS, COLUMBUS CIRCLE

Unheralded, unknown they stand today
on their small, raised platforms beside the Flag,
and drown us in their theories, irritations—
we who have gathered simply for the fun
or to kill time before a date or show—

In each earnest face we read an enormous patience,
with an almost childish joy at mouthing words,
some smooth, some sharp, like pebbles on a beach.

But their voices are shreds of agony lost
in the traffic's merciless bedlam, their frantic arms waving
puny beside the cold granite strength of buildings
leaning above them. And we turn from them quickly,
knowing all too well we have mirrored here
the farcical, tragic impotence of our age.

126

CITY HALL STREET

(For Irving Layton)

In this sweet courtyard of dirt and smells and rot
children are playing, old men rocking in their chairs,
women hanging out the ragged washings of the week.

And this goes on winter, summer, fall and spring, year after
    year,
children playing, old men rocking, women washing,
only it is other children who play, other old men who sit in
    their chairs,
other women hanging out clothes.

But this courtyard never changes—
it's still the same dirt, same rot, same smell,
same squirming, crawling tenement, same tin-roofed sweatbox
    on the lower slopes of Hell,
open sore on the gentle, smiling face of God.

TIMES SQUARE

What is supposed to impress
does not impress,
what is supposed to make my mouth gape open,
does no such foolish, no such wonderful thing.

Acres of neon, you only bore me,
high on your backdrops of night's utter darkness,
mountains of concrete, you leave me much colder
than even the stone-iron hearts who own you,
droves of unleashed traffic you only frighten me
with your mad nowhere dashes with cargoes of nothing,
great hordes of men and women, you only scare me
with the leper's gleam of death firmly set in your eyes,
locked behind the brain.

O lead me out of this boxed horror
where the world ends abruptly, where hell yawns invitingly,
O lead me out of this blackness
of bright lights and brighter, emptier faces.

RIVERDALE ZOO

I'll always remember
the dignity of the tiger
pacing the miles of his cage,
the polar bear heavy with the heat
licking his tongue so wearily
in the littered water of the pool.

In the look of each animal
no anger, no hatred,
at being in this prison,
no curse on the dumb lips,

only pity, it seemed,
deep-rooted pity,
for those faces outside
looking in with the same prisoner's eyes.

129

MAN DYING

I read it there in his eyes: *this is my last summer,*
as he sits through the daylight hours,
peak cap on his head, eyes looking straight before him,
except to turn to follow when a bird
points in his darting arrow across the grass.

Nothing the doctors know can save him now.
He sits, feeling daily the precious power
in his muscles slowly diminishing (a struggle now to light
    his pipe);
but when he looks over at me there's nothing of fear
in his eyes: death's kind look is there already.

So Jew fights Jew and Russia's sabre rattles
angrily over Europe. A jet plane with roar of hell
streaks over the housetops tingling the afternoon air.
He sits in his chair and all of it's nothing to him,
nothing at all. He's done with us now forever.

LAMBTON RIDING WOODS

Here where as children
we watched the proud riders go
up through the paths
on their strong-limbed horses,
chased the huge butterflies
over the meadows,
smelling of clover
and the burnt smell of hay:

here where we picked
the shy-eyed hepaticas,
hidden under the wet
sodden leaves on the wood slopes,
here where we ran on
the partridge and drove it
crashing and stumbling
far away in the bushes,
here where red berries
stained all our faces,
stained all our hands
as we picked them like robbers:

here where we left
some part of our childhood,
left it in keeping
for some far tomorrow,
here where our lives
met a beauty so simple,
here where the world
was a palace of wonder—
they have cut down the trees,
ploughed the grasses under,
killed every flower. . . .

There are now rows of houses
on those hills, ugly houses
with bright, ugly colours,
even uglier fences;
all the roads are muddy
and twist like bewildered snakes,
with sewer-pipes waiting
to be buried deep under
the good clean earth
now dead forever.

And next spring more rows
of these squatting toads
with more obscene colours
to pollute the countryside,

with all beauty gone
from these hillsides forever,
the memories of childhood
come crashing down,

that world of wonder,
that world of wild roses
buried with the pipes
of next year's sewers.

No more the proud riders,
no more these children. . . .

132

BRANT PLACE

The children play
in the dirt of the streets
next to factories.

The smoke from their chimneys
is almost kind
in blotting out the glare
of the blinding sun,

as the children play
in the shadow of factories
they may never escape from,

in the dirt of the streets
they may know forever.

IN PRAISE OF LONELINESS

It's loneliness of men makes poets.
The great poem is a hymn to loneliness,
a crying out in the night with no ear to listen.

This land is a breeding-ground for poets.
Here find the spawning, shining streams of poetry.
Here there is loneliness to live with, sleep with, eat with,
loneliness of streets, of the coyote.

O Mistress Loneliness, heed your worshipper.
Give him the low clear voice to be heard
in this land already loud
with the shrill cluck of the hen, the booming croak of the frog.

COURT OF GENERAL SESSIONS

This boy's face here in court
with hardness in the eyes, lips held together tightly,
facing the judge for sentence.
                    Read in it all the years
of street-gangs, corner pool-halls heavy
with smoke and bravado, dance-hall Saturday nights,
bottles bulging in suit-coats, girls ready for sex
in the borrowed car. Read there the crap games,
farce of school, hatred of cops, the strait-laced home
so respectable, so dull. Then Army years
learning to be even tougher, taught how to kill
without a second thought.
                    So are you still surprised
to see him in this stuffy city courtroom,
waiting to hear the verdict of that Law
which must condemn lest it condemn itself?

Cerberus
(1952)

LAGOONS, HANLAN'S POINT

Mornings
before the sun's liquid
spilled gradually, flooding
the island's cool cellar,
there was the boat
and the still lagoons,
the sound of my oars
the only intrusion
over cries of birds
in the marshy shallows,
loud crashing of the startled crane
rushing into air.

And in one strange,
dark, tree-hung entrance,
I followed the sound
of my heart all the way
to the reed-blocked ending,
with the pads of the lily,
thick as green-shining film,
covering the water.

136

And in another
where the sun filtered in
to probe the depths
through a lattice of branches,
I saw the skeletons
of brown ships rotting
far below in their unmarked
unknown burial ground,
wondering what strange fish
with what strange colours
swam through these palaces. . . .

A small boy
in a flat-bottomed punt
and an old pair of oars,
moving with wonder
through the antechamber
of a slowly waking world.

137

SUMMER'S GIRLS

Girls, you're simply wonderful,
you who deny yourselves meals,
live in cheap rooms,
merely to drape your young bodies
in colours that spill down your limbs,
press against your breasts,
etch sharply your thighs,
all the pigments of Easter eggs
splashing these dead streets
with summer's carnival.

Girls, we're unworthy of you,
we drab males in blues and greys.
The deep-pent life within you
sweeps by us almost madly
like cars on a speedway,
and as we watch, spellbound,
you turn to wave at us,
gathering us up
in your whirlwind race
we never quite understand.

138

SCOUDOUC: THAT LOST YEAR

(No. 4 Repair Depot, RCAF)

Whatever we sought or dreamed of in a name
it wasn't here. Name for a mile of runways
the four turns of the wind; junk-pile of aircraft—
Dakota, Canso, Hudson and Ventura—
jammed in the mud that quagmired everywhere.

Here a whole year of our lives died quietly
without rebellion, fuss. Rebel against what?
Kick against stone walls? The Service held us tight
in its steel-firm fist. One drank poison, died,
another lost reason. The rest of us, cowed sheep,
cursed your name under our breath, waited quietly
for some miracle of deliverance; while engines shook our sleep
with unholy music, while the sergeants roared,
and feet marched up the road and down again....

139

LIGHTS AND SHADOWS

Casa Loma's lights blazing,
sleek cars gliding up to unload
the dancers of the evening.

(Go on, Jim Reaney,
you finish it perhaps with a few witches
brewing one monstrous potion
in the middle of the Great Hall),

while I go up this street
to the private nursing-home
with all the windows shut tight
against the summer evening breezes,

to your drawn face on its pillow,
and talk of meaningless trifles
while those twin knives inside you
cut away at your living,

both of us waiting for the nurse
to come with some dope
to relax the edges
of your beautiful pain:

O knives be still
for a few precious minutes!

(Go on, Jim Reaney,
you finish it maybe
with a lightning, fanciful
sally at the moon).

THE TWENTY-FIFTH OF DECEMBER

Stack the windows high
till they almost crack,
heap up the monumental
junk-pile of Christmas;

forty-nine price-tags
and a picture of Santa Claus,
fifty-nine price tags
and a barber-pole candy-cane;

hark the herald angels sing
all sales final,
peace on earth, mercy
to all cash customers;

O little town of Bethlehem
ONLY TWO MORE SHOPPING DAYS,
Noel, Noel,
scotch pines, $2.50;

sixty-nine price-tags
and a tinsel-coloured sky,
Good King Wenceslas
in the bargain basement.

Merry Christmas,
suckers.

SELF-PORTRAIT FROM THE YEAR 1952

In this first year of the Atom Death
what is in store for you, poet, my poet?
Hair greying fast, belly softening faster,
your days of romance well behind you, Great Lover.

Turning the crank of a mimeograph
in a basement cellar to produce yet another
"little magazine" perhaps fifty will read through,
twenty remember (and with luck) five will learn from.

Engaged through the week at Usura,
and kidding yourself it doesn't leave
the marks of its uselessness upon you.

Weekends spent spewing great vomits of poetry
returned with short pencilling by editors:
"Try us again some other year."

Yet a kind of stubbornness in the blood
and a wife who refuses to recognize genius,
should carry you fortified, still somehow alive,
through the death and dying of a generation.

142

O MIGHTY RIVER

Faces were flowing by me,
tossed, twisted in the street swell,
thrown against the shoal rocks of bar-stools,
dashed against the wrecks of armless mannequins.

Faces were showered at my eyes,
pimps, whores, thieves, saints and lovers—
strange loot of Christ and the devil
flashed against a montage of terror. . . .

O mighty river of Yonge Street,
rinse through and cleanse me,
wash in a suds of beer spills and cigarette ash,
dry with the scorched heat of belly-dancers;

with always the drone from the all-night mission
cry of ten lost foghorns deafening my ears.

143

ROLLER-SKATE MAN

A freak of the city,
little man with big head,
shrivelled body, stumps of legs
clamped to a square of wood
running on roller-skate wheels.

Leather gloves on his hands
because the Queen Street pavements
are rough when your hands are paddles,
and your strange craft speeds between
silk-stockinged legs and extravagant
pleats over elevator shoes,

steering through the old familiar waters
of spit, old butts, chewed-up gum,
flotsam among the jetsam of your world.

144

THE MAN WHO FINDS HIS SON HAS BECOME
A THIEF

Storming into the store at first angry
at the accusation, believing whole-heartedly
the words of his young one who's told him
I didn't steal anything, honest. . . .

Then somehow becoming calmer, seeing that anger
won't help now at all, listening even patiently
as the others' evidence unfolds so painfully slow.

Then gradually seeing that evidence
almost as if inch by inch tightening around the neck
of his son, at first circumstantial, then gathering sure damage,
until he's aware of guilt's ugly odour seeping
into his nostrils, choking and horrible to bear.

Now suddenly feeling sick and alone and afraid,
as if some unseen hand had slapped his face
again and again, for no reason whatsoever; desperately wanting
to rush out into the street, the night, the darkness, anywhere
    to hide
the pain that must show to these strangers,
and even more than that, the fear, his fear. . . .

It must be like this.
It could hardly be otherwise.

LITTER OF THE LATE LAST ROSE

Litter of the late last rose
rough-handled by the wind
and laid there on the grass,

in the short sundial sweep
of your life, happy interval
between bloom and the beginning of decay,

I read my own life
swiftly climbing now to its zenith.

146

STEEL PLANT SATURDAY NIGHT

Sweet perfume of benzine, coal-tar,
smell of burning flesh from the coke ovens—
black, burning flesh of the Negroes living in rat-hutches
under the flash and flare-up of the open hearth,
black flesh slowly turned on the spit of death
and oblivion, steel fork of the white boss
plunged in from time to time to test
the progress of certain agony.

While the face of the Wurlitzer
in the corner hamburger joint is the gleaming giant eye
of night blinking through the peeling store-fronts,
soot-washed stoops, cracked windows, broken doors,
it smirks and laughs right out loud
at the soldier fingering the twelve-year-old
deep in the porch's shadow, then really splits a gut
watching old grandpa in his once-white nightshirt
barely making it to the back door
before he lets fly. . . .

All this to the low-pitched rumble
of the rolling-mill, rising like a crazy moan
from the lips of the tormented;
while in the movie-house heaven
(blacks in the balcony only),
the shine and sparkle of the Pacific glows,
the blue of untroubled water overpowers—here love
is both noble and unforced. . . .

The girl on the porch bites back the pain;
the drunk retches; and always the Wurlitzer
booms on and on and on. . . .

SALUTE TO BOBBY HACKETT

One of his fingers holds a ring
and that fat ring glows brilliantly,
almost outshines the way the light
above the happy bandstand catches
the golden sparkle of his horn.

But nothing shines so or can outshine
the sound, the joyous summoning,
pushing its way across this room
of faces hard or flushed or gay—

and it may yet transform them all
into a mood for listening
to what the music laughs or cries
through all the chatter, smoke and noise,
through all the feigned indifference
to wonder knocking at their ears.

THE LILAC POEM

Before lilac-time is over and each fragrant branch
becomes a shrunken stalk hanging down very limp and dead,
I want to write a poem about lilacs and their beauty
brief and star-shining as a young girl's beauty.

Because there's so much made of strength and wealth and
    power,
because the little things are often lost in this world,
I write this poem about lilacs knowing well that both
are this day's only: tomorrow they will lie forgotten.

FREAK SHOW

Perhaps some day the Professor's fleas may pull
in gilded coach the Thinnest Man in the World
together with his smiling bride the Crocodile Girl
up to the church doors where the Armless Woman
waits to toss confetti with her skilful toes;

and together with their best man the Tattooed Giant
and their bridesmaid the demure Leopard Girl,
they'll walk altarward with the music of the Bearded Brothers
ringing in their ears, where the King of the Midgets,
modest JP, will perform the nuptials;

with their friend the Half Man puffing calmly on his cigar
in the front row of guests, and above all else
the impatient clamour of flea-hoofs
sounding ever so faintly outside on the cobblestones.

COAL PILES, ASHBRIDGE'S BAY

Blacker than any night these stretch smooth shadows
into the oil-slicked water, ghost-like, huge.
Tonight this sky's the Devil's, these his meadows,
gained by who knows what sooty subterfuge?

AFTERNOON BY THE OUSE

(For Nathan Ralph)

First we came out of the bustling echo-chamber
of York station, then walked through centuries'-old streets.
Next came the bridge, the Ouse below brown, sluggish, dead,
then more streets narrowing.
                        It was in that park
where the gates closed at five, down by the river,
that we sat in the shade on the long grass and talked
of books, poetry and war. The typed pages of your novel
lay strewn out beside us, sure symbol of silence,
cunning and, above all, exile. O we had
great dreams that day, great future dreams,
and dreams are so easy three thousand miles from home,
almost too-rich fare for over-starved appetites. . . .

Now tell me, where are those dreams,
eye-straining bank clerk, alert seller of trinkets?
Where's all that stuff we pulled then
from that warm, so peaceful Yorkshire sky?
Where's that brash, impetuous brag of youth
we wore then like tunics, that damn-them-all scorn
flashing like polished cap badges?
Tell me, is it gone now, all of it,
or does part of it still linger somewhere in our heads,
waiting for better times, the event sudden like gold?
Or simply an afternoon like that by the Ouse,
when, through the late sunshine, over long grass growing,
youth will come walking again?

STORM IN NOVEMBER

The storm begun tonight
still rages toward its height,
wind, darkness now combined
against what it may find
lost, blinded, shelterless,
man's usual distress.

Now safe inside we know
the morning light will show
tree branches torn and spread
like bodies of the dead,
a world subdued and white
to balance off the night.

TO AN ANTI-SEMITE

Kike, yid bitch she is to you,
unspeakably lewd, mother of all evil—

but to me she is soft-spoken, kind,
a girl undressing down by the brown summer waters
of the Little Jesus River, plunging in

to wash from her body all the dirt of New York,
all the filth of you and those other spineless rats
of the Great Terrible City, sick, tormented, afraid,
as you slide and scramble on the endless garbage dumps
    of your mind.

LONDON RENDEZVOUS

(For Don)

. . . Later that night in a pub
at Shepherd's Bush made our last stand.
Your leave was shot and the train
stood waiting at Waterloo.
So we pledged the past, then saluted
the future with a row of pints;
but closing-time came, found us still
at our table with much beer to drink,
and an ugly, old cross-eyed slut
standing over us hefty and mean,
with her tired singsong of a phrase,
"Time, now, please, gentlemen, time—"

(O at that moment how we knew
that this old slut was really the War,
her filthy finger up both our lives,
but saw she was too damn big
for us to be able to throw,
so got up slowly from the table
and soberly walked out the door. . . .)

Then the Tube flashed, a thousand lights roared,
and somehow the evil-hissing tomb
of Waterloo Station again,
our hands making futile gestures
that they'd made at least twice before,

then darkness swallowed you up,
Europe took you back again to mould
in the shape of her giant will,
and I walked out of Waterloo alone
like a lost drunk man and down
the sprawling darknesses of streets,
still stranger in a stranger land.

MEMO TO THE HUMAN RACE

The chances of survival on this earth
are perhaps one to three now
this year of the atom. Do not increase them
by adding that strange word *love*
to your vocabulary.

153

Shake Hands with
the Hangman
(1953)

JAZZ CONCERT, MASSEY HALL

You'll blow the dusty top off this emporium,
blow it right off, float it gently up and over
Yonge Street:
            you, Rex, with those fat cheeks,
you, Illinois, greased and dapper, you, old Buck Clayton,
you, soaring Hawk:
            all this noisy crew bringing
their Manhattan madness up here where we like it quiet
(but never the sober, death-quiet our elders have given it!)

O faces are shining, are happy
with your beat, your blowings of fire,
O everything's got a fever,
everything, everyone.

So don't stop, horns, don't stop, trombones,
bass keep thumping cleanly, piano tinkling,

and have another try at that roof.

156

DEATH OF THE DAWN PATROL

(Christmas Day, 1943)

When you were turning comfortably in your bed
with no thought of waking ... suddenly the starboard engine
cut out cold and down she went
like a stone dropped in a well,
with only two hundred feet before the trees. . . .

When you were reaching for another drink
beside the comfortable fire ... the search-party found
what they really hadn't expected—part of an arm.
All the other pieces were too small, too much
like chewed-up meat to look like pieces of boys.

157

SOFTLY AS FIRST LEAVES FALL

Softly as first leaves fall
on a late September evening
when there's no wind or cold
or any sign of death,
and they float with no reluctance
down to the waiting earth:

landing almost as softly
as our first kiss taken,
(it also unexpected,
drifting in from those meadows of chance),

leaving me lost
between earth and heaven,
seeking out that distant
throbbing airport of your heart.

ICICLE OUTSIDE THE BARRACKS

An icicle tall as a man
hangs outside our window,
sharp as the killer's point
of our madman's war,

waiting the first
warm day to leap
and sever the white
soft breasts of the snow.

SLEEP TORONTO

Sleep city sleep
push the last dead drunks into the cells of oblivion,
chase the last chilled street-walker back to her rooming-house,
bed the last derelict in the overnight cot of the mission;

then sleep from the putrid Don to the puny Humber,
sleep from Hog's Hollow all the way to the lake cold and dark,
sleep down in Cabbagetown, sleep up in Forest Hill,
sleep soundly on the beds of gold, the bunks of hunger.

Sleep on, knowing well you're both spendthrift and miser,
bigoted, hypocrite, little wise, much foolish,
sleep with the dreams of profits, mergers, margins,
sleep with the dreams of garbage-dump and dole.

Sleep city sleep
your Yonge Street narrow as the hearts that own you.

LET ME ALWAYS REMEMBER

Let me always remember
when I'd like to curse these people—
these dull, empty-seeming faces—

that they have the same dreams,
same hopes, same desires,
same fears, same frustrations.

O even when they laugh
and won't hear me,
let me always remember
that I too came from them.

QUESTION FOR A SOLDIER

How many dead will you have to see in a war
before you'll know it's Death that you're fighting for?

THREE WAYS OF LOOKING AT NEW YORK

1

A thousand bars have neon on fire tonight;
down in Times Square the miracle billboard mouth
blows smoke-rings into the summer-heavy air.

Before Central Park hotels one long parade
of limousines disgorging tails and furs.

(City with a price
everyone pays in time)

2

New York
face of a young Negro
in a tavern off Amsterdam Avenue,
seeing death his own reflection
in a glass of bitter bourbon.

(City with a price
everyone pays in time)

161

3

New York
oil-slick filthy
as your East River cesspool,
majestic as your Hudson's sunset gold,
all of you smells of faded, hand-worn money,
all of you lost in a forest of gleaming bills,
skyscrapers buried under a fine black rain of dollars.

(City with a price
everyone pays in time)

I WATCHED A BIRD

I watched a bird blown down the sky
like some poor thing without control,
dipping, then swerving here and there,
with wings spread wide and motionless.

I watched a bird tossed down the wind
that never fought or uttered cry,
surrendered to that boundless air,
caught up in that great mystery.

TROOPSHIP OUTSIDE HALIFAX HARBOUR

Our ship moves slowly through the fog
with a cat-creeping slowness.
Nothing but this screen of fog
for our eyes, our hearts to cling to.

Now at intervals the sudden burp
of our fog-horn.

We crowd the rails,
breathe in the too-damp air,
then wait in the silent way we've learned
(as only men like us could ever learn
the dumb, patient faith of waiting):

thinking: somewhere out there is home. . . .

163

WHERE THE BLUE HORSES

The street is quiet,
any noise through the wall is stilled,
our little cat curled up on the kitchen chair,
the radio finally off,
milk bottles placed outside the door.

So for now
nothing but sleep and dreams and thoughts of sleep,
not even love keep us awake tonight,

as we sink into that strange land
where the blue horses toss
riderless and proud.

SHY ONE, CAUTIOUS ONE

I want to wound your white flesh,
cover it with the bruises of my lips,
then lance it through and through
with the wild thrust of my loving.

Shy one, cautious one,
this is no time for shyness,
no year for any caution.

From your slim waist to your thighs
curving like waterfalls I read there
poems more wonderful than any starlight
or moonlight stained by no war or the hate of men.

THE SENATOR GOES HOME

Finally hoisted
by four struggling pairs of hands
onto the fourth sleeping-car
of the Ocean Limited
only minutes before departure-time,

the senator slumped down beside us,
and all that evening
while the train roared or snorted
like an angry thing,
he drank our rye,
told dirty jokes,
followed every passing woman
with his beady eyes.

Was lifted finally
up into his berth,
then kept us awake
for an hour with his snoring.

Then reappeared all smiles
at breakfast next morning,
to expound the virtues
of constitutional government
halfway through New Brunswick.

165

YONGE STREET BAR

The lighting's so arranged in here
with each piled-up row of bottles
such a shimmer-haze of blue,
that you can almost imagine
you're sitting in a place far away
from this city and its dead;

almost believe you're not in a crowded late bar
phony from its chrome to its overplush furniture,
clip-joint of watered drinks, cheap women, rummy playboys.

Really, there's something almost beautiful,
almost good, almost child-like,
the way these bottles seem to glow
like so many blue fairy lights!

OUR WORLD IN WINTER

Darling, look at the snow
settling on our world out there,
sifted through the dark earth places
with the pureness of heaven.

Brushed against every tree,
its touch almost silk-like,
wrapping the last torn leaf
in the folds of compassion.

Covering the stiffened-cold robin
morning left at our door
with such a fine grave-cloth
that death seems no evil,

only swift, incidental,
as snow shifting on the roof.

167

QUIET EVENING

No lust tonight in my body
I lie with you on this bed,
and your nearness is enough,
the warm slight sigh of your breathing
is enough, is all to me.

Words we don't speak
flutter through our heads like hands touching,
lips meeting.

And over us, hovering
with the slow soft rustle of his wings,
sleep is waiting patiently, lovingly,
to lead us by the arm
into that far green valley of his keeping.

168

PARADE OF THE TOYS

Streets and streetcars all crowded with children
going downtown to see their Santa Claus
and all twelve prancing reindeer
as they ride to their home away from home.

Drink it all in, little eyes,
little ears, little hearts,
believe in it as you've never
believed anything before!

Because it won't last very long—
and before you know it they'll shatter
every dream you ever had,
and there won't be Santa anywhere

but only windows piled with junk,
with happy drunks at every corner,
and grown people crying like children
in a world they don't know anymore.

YOU ARE

You are my happy summer,
my flaring rocket
soaring up into a sky now darkening,
lighting this grey impenetrable city
with the colours of your eyes, your hair, your lips.

O you are my carnival, my Sunnyside
of roller-coasters, popcorn, nervous lights,
you are that solitary tree outside my window
shining from warmth and rain, erect and proud,
tossing high her head into the morning wind.

ON THE ESPLANADE

Behind us the city's one good hotel
where tailor-made dummies of officers
plan the evening's boredom in the lobby's well-lighted
    vacuum.

Down the slope before us the docks, then the black-crêpe
    water
stretching to where a few mean shore lights
tickle the darkness.

On the ship anchored under us
a welder throws slender lighthouse flashes
on and off, off and on.

Cool winds stalk the harbour now,
I shiver against you once or twice.
Your lips are painted lush red,
not black, not ghostly violet,
life to kiss, and warm,
O how warm they are!

Here am I, an unbelieving Lazarus
suddenly come alive from the dead,
and twice reborn to your slightest touching!

171

THE SOUND

Listen—that sound again—
just beyond the edge
of our door a stir
of leaves falling in the night,
drifting, sifting so softly down
to the already-littered earth,
you'd think they were totally unaware
of the final severing,
this sad parting in the autumn dark.

Nothing anywhere so fine tonight
as this sweet moving
from life into death.

172

CAPE BRETON SUMMER EVENING

The band really isn't worth a damn,
still, the sweat is working through your powder,
through the starch of my carefully ironed shirt.

Outside the moon
sends old ghosts to walk a thoroughfare of gold
across the water white beach to driftwood shore.
Now a breeze skims over,
smelling deep lake, dark pine branch.

Thank God for intermissions!

Our limbs ache with desire, a heat's in our blood,
as we climb the wood-road till the forest takes us,
leaving the over-loud lights, the idle chattering,
and our friends of the dance-floor guzzling pop and piercing
the thin yielding skin of hot-dogs.

THE MYSTERY

O why can't all the world
move toward its golden centre
just as we move closer, surer,
to our dream of love?

And people with the beautiful bodies given them—
how is it they have time left to cheat and kill
in any name, for any cause righteous or evil,

now it is summer when the days are warm
and the night air shaken with the silver of little bells?

173

DEATH WATCH

Far beyond the nurses' residence,
stretched out like a still-warm corpse,

my summer-sweating city
hazy now with lights
on the most barren alleys,
the emptiest of streets.

Precisely each minute
the fog-horn from the Island
curses the stubborn fog
night-long without end.

In this hospital room
to the hornet's hum
of an electric fan,
my uncle breathes desperately
in his hypoed sleep.

Our eyes, slowly lidded
more and more with tiredness,
wait for his dying.

174

GRADUATION PARTY, RCAF

The Jewish boy's drunk, the ones who do not drink are drunk,
our corporals even are drunk; there's mad singing and the
    sergeant shouting
Canadienne with a maximum of gestures. And all the time
the bartenders with slick white jackets
smile broadly, fingers punching cash-register music.

I went outside a while ago
to breathe in some fresh, cold air. Half-shrouded by night,
the hill made a wild swoop downward
behind the hotel. At the bottom were lights, soon to fade,
of the town. The lake was somewhere near,
you could sense it almost, but the dark had hidden it.
My breath rose in long thin streamers
up toward the stars and the moon, the snow felt crisp and dry
under my feet, wind cold, freshening in from the lake.

The laughter of the boys inside
sounded suddenly harsh, almost foreign. Still, I came back in
to their loud, youthful, restless gaiety that seemed to be striving
    madly
to chase loneliness away till dawn, to lock darkness up in
    some far room,
to keep the heart singing, tongue sparkling, eyes shining,
the mind leaping higher, higher, higher,

to hide death's hand in long wild robes of madness.

175

THE MOTHER

The cat walks easily,
belly sagging with kittens,
between the feet
of the sailors and whores.

Be careful, mother,
for their boots are sharp,
and they have little love left
for even their own kind.

AIRMAN COMING OUT OF A DREAM

First we'd stepped off the Hanlan's Point ferry,
then, as the passengers scattered,
moved quickly past the loud-mouthed amusement-park
and begun to walk under the willows
along a path beside a motionless lagoon
(each tree a twisted trunk bowed down with branches
of shivering greenness, and through them the night sky,
even flashes now and then of the moon).

And as we walked arm-in-arm together
I'd been wondering for more than the first time
what made your hands so puppy-soft, so warm. . . .
Then the siren wailed, droned, and wailed again,
and through our barrack-room the sound
of all the boys slowly coming out of their dreams right
    behind me.

THE WAY IT COULD HAVE BEEN

Say a night like tonight,
street dark, all houses silent,
a few snowflakes sifting down.

You must have slowly walked along this sidewalk,
then onto the bridge over the steep ravine.
Far, far below, lights stretching weakly out
winked up at you, as you stood leaning over,
watching perhaps with too-great fascination
their strangely-evil hypnotic glow.

                                    Suddenly
took a deep breath, as I imagine it,
deep enough to last you almost forever,
then quickly looked both ways to be certain
nobody was watching. Then no doubt
you almost sprang up on the guard-rail.

After which you jumped.

177

THE URGE

Spring drives them eagerly out into the street,
propelled by a breathless urge they could never explain,
but which we might probably guess is desire to meet
new dreams, new faces (and without wishing it), new pain.

The rich, the poor, the crippled and the blind
are one tonight with the young girls and the strutting boys,
all groping for something lost they may never find
in the drab of the street, in the dirt, in the smoke, in the noise.

LOVERS

It's simply wonderful to watch them:
they're so much in love with each other
that they're always embarrassing the rest of us—
as when she'll lean over, kiss him very suddenly,
or he'll dig his lips almost hungrily into her neck,
finish up by running both hands quickly over her breasts—

then they'll both look up—she with her innocent eyes
that seem to have wakened from a kind of sleep;
he with a shaking back of his wavy hair,
the laughing soul of Satan mirroring his smile.

O and when they walk out with us
you can almost sense in their hurrying closeness of movement,
that they want to outdistance us, lose us quickly,
and hurrying home wrap their bodies achingly together,
dive out and twist up above Mount Royal and the stars.

THAT FACE, THAT HAND

As we came down the walk from the hospital
we knew both followed us. . . . How did we know?
We didn't really, only sensed it—
but then something forced us to turn, to look up—
and there at a fifth-floor window a childish face
and beside it a hand waving us goodbye.

And of course we waved back to that face,
that hand, both so dwarfed in the climb
of huge buildings, myriad room lights, even giant darkness,
then walked slowly on together.

But more than a year later now
I still see that face, that hand,
framed in a small square of light in a prison without any bars,
both with the look of the helpless, the lost. O surely never
more helpless or lost the human spirit trapped
up behind that window! Denied the life flowing by
in the street below—sad, yes, lewd and loud, certainly—
but still with life's movement, the promise of the dream!

That face to me will always be framed up there,
that hand to me will always be waving its goodbye. . . .

179

AT THE CENOTAPH

Very cold here this morning with rain. Time now
for a bowing of heads, the placing of wreaths on the cenotaphs,
time now for the pat speech together with its measure
of carefully ladled-out, well controlled emotion.

Even time to twist the nightmare moment of dying
into another *dulce et decorum est.* . . .

Well, they won't stir now after so many years of sleeping,
the dead will not speak now after these years of silence.
Not by any sign here today will you know they are other
     than dust.
Their bones are deep in the earth: those bones will stay there.

So say your piece quickly and get in out of the rain
and the cold and the smell of your slime
hanging in the air at the cenotaphs.

ON THE WAY TO A WAR

After the third or fourth time
of easing myself down
from my third-tier bunk,
then climbing the twenty steel steps
on iron-weighted legs
to the head on the next deck above,

I dragged up an old orange crate
lying somehow mysteriously there,
and sat limp for most of the night
listening to the suck-gurgle toilets—
their sound the senseless clack
of our patriotic poets—

Except, that is, when I knelt or squatted
in worship before the Great White Bowl,
its cool porcelain touch at that moment
much dearer to me by far
than all the girls back in Toronto!

With all the time in the world
to reflect on the many unexpected ways
the dignity of a man is dragged down,
laughed at, fouled upon,
to the gently flushed toilet-bowl laughter
of the one-and-ninety heavenly angels.

MONTREAL AFTER DARK

Endless streets of the neon
red
green
blue
winking

All the bars filled
all the glasses brimming
all the bands frantic
all the taxis taken
all the women beautiful
all the rooms taken

It must be sad
even awkward to be poor. . . .

But then we can't
all be rich,
n'est-ce pas?

MIRROR OF THE PAST

Parked on this lonely road tonight,
looking down the hill below, where boys
go through scrambled motions of hockey
under the floodlights of the county rink,

no doubt about it we see ourselves
only a short ten years back boys such as these,
when games loomed so large in our lives—
delight in the wrist-steered puck, tired muscles
aching with precious victory, inglorious defeat.

Torture of women unknown then, the restlessness
that has us now gripped by the throat (hangover
of war and uniforms), still undreamed of, that anger
at the smallness of our lives, caged antics
of home to office to home not yet horizoned.

How innocent their world!·
(Our world of the early years),
how complete, how self-sufficient,
rosy-red!

The bottle's top comes expertly off
first crack, and we waste no time
getting into this second crock of gin,

still enviously watching the darting figures below,
our lost youth racing there, fearless, exulting!

THE BOURGEOIS CHILD

I might have been a slum child,
I might have learned to swear and steal,
I might have learned to drink and whore.

But I was raised a good bourgeois child
so it has taken me a little longer.

184

LEAVING MONTREAL

What a day to be leaving!

Sun blinding the windows
of old Durocher Street,
traffic gleaming up on Sherbrooke,
crowds colouring St. Catherine,
the mountain reborn
in a riot of leaves,
a swift torrent of grasses!

There is something very evil
about trains and stations,
each clock has the look
of an arch-conspirator.

And always the thought
that the end of this journey
is Toronto and drabness,
is Toronto and its slow death
in wait there to smother me,

O waiting to choke me
with tender, treacherous fingers!

GOODBYE

Once more we are torn from each other
as bark is torn from over-delicate trees.

When we'll meet again
they say no-one knows,
not even heaven's riders.

But this is one time
the smart ones are wrong
right up to the level
of their fat, polished necks:

I tell you I'll meet you,
see your face,
hear your voice shaking silver bells,
every time I look at a sky-arched tree
standing poised on a single leg,
every time a star lances through the darkness,
every time a flower
pushes through the mud.

Every time that beauty
gladness is.

ADVICE FOR A CRITIC

Go pick your nose
over someone else's verse,

saving all your snot
to write your own epitaph.

DOWNTOWN CORNER NEWSSTAND

It will take death to move you from this corner,
for it's become your world and you its unshaved,
bleary-eyed, foot-stamping king.

In winter you curse the cold, huddled in your coat from the
    wind,
then fry in summer like an egg hopping in a pan,
and always that whining voice, those nervous-flinging arms,
the red face, shifting eyes watching, waiting
under the grimy cap for God knows what to happen.

But nothing ever does; downtown Toronto
goes to sleep and wakes the next morning
always the same, except a little dirtier,
as you stand with your armful of *Stars* and *Telys*,
the peak of your cap well down against the sun,
and all the city's restless, seething river
surges up around you, but never once
do you plunge in its flood to be carried or tossed away—

but reappear always, beard longer than ever, nose running,
to catch the noon editions at King and Bay.

DIRGE FOR THE NEW WORLD

Hitler is dead,
that has been clearly established.
Il Duce with him,
there's even a noose to prove it.

But war isn't dead,
war is very much alive,
hate flares on every street,
love is something in the movies
or the cheap hotel room,
and only war is great,
only war is feared.
Christ and Lenin have been crucified
on the selfsame bloody cross.
Nobody wants to think or listen
so the bodies will have to pile up again.
The world is rotten but still
we lick at its stinking corpse,
the world is sick and dying
but we think it will live again.

This is not despair, only truth,
this is not a wail but a warning.
O world without love, only death,
O world without peace, only war,
O world with only a Bomb
to show for all our sweat and our blood!

BRIDGE OVER THE DON

Why does your loneliness surge up,
why does that ugliness, despair,
hit you squarely between the eyes?

Is it because you stand on a bridge late at night,
because you keep looking down at the darkened water,
because your eyes move out into even greater darkness?

Haven't you seen the river before,
don't you know it runs and smells like a sewer,
haven't you choked before this on the smoke from these
    factories
looking in the night like the tombs of uneasy ghosts?

Why do you come to get cheered up here
with three hotels down the block
and a jitterbug dancehall?
Don't you know people can get melancholy, go even queer,
standing like you are, just looking out ahead at the darkness,

trying to find some truth, even beauty,
where beauty and truth have been burned out, slugged out,
given the gate forever?

THE TASTE OF THEIR WAR

The taste of their war
so heavy in my mouth,
choking, unclean thing,

which I spit now in the faces
of those who twist laws
of those who make bombs
of those who shape guns
of those who flame men's hate
of those who kill children
of those who murder love
of those who finally pierce my heart.

NE PASSEZ PAS

(For Pat and Miriam)

NE PASSEZ PAS SUR LE GAZON
and if you're a Jew
keep off our beaches
and if you're a Jew
keep off our golf-courses,
and if you're a Jew . . .

NE PASSEZ PAS

(Does their good Mary know this?)

FOOTNOTE TO MR. MASSEY'S REPORT

Culture—
that word should stick in your throats—

Something you can't buy
with your filthy, useless money,
something you can't produce
like a crop of mushrooms
at your grovelling universities . . .

Not so much a report
as a small
very irritating rattle.

191

GERRARD STREET EAST

The dingy movie will be emptying soon,
lights of the beverage-room click out, with floors swept and
    washed, chairs carefully piled,
the door of the pool-hall slammed shut, each shining green
    table asleep, click of ball striking ball silent now,
and then the last restaurant will close, chime of cash-register
    over, carefully polished urn gleaming faintly in the darkness.

Then, only then will the late last walker know himself alone,
friendless, with no place to go,
then and only then will his heart seem to slowly turn to stone,

as one with peeling store-fronts, settling houses, smelly alleys,
the unswept sidewalks raising a little dust or a piece of old
    newspaper
as the night wind breathes softly, lovingly, on all of it.

192

SPRING EVENING IN ANOTHER COUNTRY

(Yorkshire, 1945)

Something crossed the sky outside my window,
but it was only a bird,
not one of our bombers approaching circuit,
its engines roaring out gladness.

The evening was quiet
except for some rooks in the trees
beyond the last barrack-block, with every field
edging the base more beautiful
in the late last sun than even much earlier
when I'd walked from Topcliffe to Thirsk
through the morning heat, fields on each side of the road
wet with dew and green, glistening green, and showing lambs
like small rolls of fluff, heads down, busy in the grass....

So tonight no roaring out of aircraft,
no sound of war anywhere,
the strange, perfect wonder of it all!

ROOM AT THE TOP OF THE STAIRS

(For Margaret Avison)

Five-o'clock crowds,
policemen's whistles
whipping waves
of motors, lights
across
black intersections.

Noise grates,
rain mocks
these faces bleared
as never before. . . .

Then to come down
still street
to hid house,
climbing to a room
where the dim one light
breathes peace,
and the great untroubled
voice of poetry
is all.

194

THE BULL-PEN

(RCAF Manning Depot, Toronto)

This is the bull-pen,
a thousand boys sleep here,

coughing at night
with a sound no bull
could possibly achieve.

TO THE NATIONAL ASSEMBLY TO SAVE PEACE

Picture me a bird,
picture me a dove,
the same beautiful creature
(by Picasso)
you've defiled by printing
on your letterhead.

Then watch me wing over
to explode on your platform of deception
the dreaded A-bomb of truth.

195

RETREAD

(No. 4 Repair Depot, RCAF)

When the asthma hits him bad
in the night I often wonder
if he'll get his breath again,
but he somehow always does;

and exactly at six AM
there's the sound of a bottle
being opened on the edge
of the bunk bed below me,

and I know it's Jim right on schedule,
starting work on last night's hangover
from payday at the wet canteen.

Two quarts into him by seven
and he'll be up, shaved, good as new,
for eight-o'clock morning parade,

or at least as new
as anyone can expect
from forty-nine years
and two lousy wars!

SUMMER AFTERNOON AT CHARLEMAGNE

Strange now what remains most
from that afternoon—

not the magazines fresh from New York
(poetry's latest salvation),
not the volleyball game,
the sprawls, falls, contortions,
not even the country supper,
heaped dishes, smooth white cloth
spread on the picnic table;

but instead the sudden
storm-signals of onslaught
from the rain's grey Uhlans,
moving from one planned
objective to another,
nearer, always nearer,
sullenly, relentlessly,
advancing, advancing. . . .

So that with the first drops
we ran like people trapped,
gathering tables, chairs, dishes,
in one crazy last effort,

to finally stand, soaked and breathless,
on that cottage verandah,
watching the triumphant
march-past of the invader.

197

THE NATURE OF POETRY

Poems should never be written
(so you tell me)
about a white-haired man
carrying bundles of old newspapers
(bent back covered with the strips
of a one-time shirt)
from one dusty lane to another.

Instead (you still tell me)
make them
out of dark-haired young women
with cooing-dove breasts
sheathed in dresses that drown them
in pools of the rainbow.

But I write both

One for my pleasure
one for my pain

One from guilt
the other from desire

(which no-one reads
anyway)

198

DREAM NEAR MIDNIGHT

If some night when the barrack lights are out,
and even the restless ones sleep like the dead,
you'd creep between the breathing tiers and up
into the warm, tight attic of my bed,

your breasts would melt my chest as never before,
your lips would start the sweat along my thighs,
with all my trembling manhood kneeling down
before your flower opening its eyes!

DISSECTION

Being quite dead, a poet so-called,
and Canadian to boot, they had him hauled
to the nearest lab and the very next day
sliced down the middle to find how he got that way.

Then wished they hadn't. For this man had died
many years before; what they looked at inside
was now only a shell, a decayed, empty shell
of what he'd once been before he'd gone all to hell.

The brains, the guts, the heart had been long since flushed
clean as a whistle—still, somehow the words had gushed
in a seemingly marvellous, inexhaustible flow
until the body's rebellion—how about us when we go?

THE IMPULSE

Caught in an eddy of crosswinds,
blown downward, shot upward,
as if undecided like a woman
with two bold lovers,

suspended between narrow buildings,
riding high above the Bay Street traffic,

a piece of old newspaper,
lost, lonely gull,
suddenly took heart
and acting on an impulse
wheeled abruptly out of sight
around Richmond Street corner.

200

NOT WHOLLY LOST

John warns me of nostalgia
and I suppose he's right,
but what the hell—

why are poems made but for celebration
of our time here on earth, the years behind
and ahead of us? And I for one will leave
all the future to others and plunge gladly back
into the mist of old ghosts and places
where these appear . . .
                                    scarlet flame of Dosco's
open-hearth hell behind the jail; stench of coke-ovens;
poverty naked as the Newfie girl under her dress
that cold November; fish-smell and ocean scum
at North Sydney piers; lobster on the half-shell
in Cormier's; the movie where fifty was a crowd; and on from
    Shediac
the warm sands, blue waters of the Point, where summer
    seemed over
before it had really begun, and our youth with it,
for that year anyway. But there was another year
and another summer (thank God there was always another!).
Remember, we never did find any clams
but drank that bottle of rum on the shell-heavy sands of
    Buctouche,
coming back to camp hungry.
                                    And in yet another year
and in a strange new country—what better days were there
than mornings on the Bournemouth cliffs, blue above and
    below,
each outshining the other. Or nights walking Yorkshire roads,
great trees on either side, good smell of hay from the fields. . . .

We'll never do the things now we did then,
we've grown older, much too serious. What we did once
for the plain simple hell of it we'll not do again in any year;
but we did them once—those things are not wholly lost—
they linger on in the heart, in the mind, like a lost girl or a song,
and nothing can take them from us or change them
unless it is death.

THE GIRL IN THE GUMBO

Your nose may be a little long,
but no-one cares too much
in a place like this, do they?

Just the same I wish someone
would come in here right now,
sit down and bargain,
then take you quickly away
to your room or wherever you do business,

because I can't stand to look
any more at your face with its proud
bravado of a look that conceals
the way I think you'd simply like to cry,
head buried deep in your arms.

I also know you'd probably say
pity is something that won't buy make-up
or clothes or a better apartment,
and so is really useless to you now,

a phony twenty taken in exchange
for your body's frank, vibrant giving.

KEW BEACH REVISITED

1940
year of my first big love,
kid stuff, but wonderful.
Riding out here from the West End
a long eight miles every night,
to hurl back on two-AM Queen Street,
swaying streetcar racing the moon.

The beach very nice then,
wide, with the sand white and clean.
We'd lie there long after the heat
of the summer sun had drained out of it.
Most of all I remember some trees
back near the boardwalk, a cool wind onshore
swaying the branches, the thick, green leaves.

1952
the beach now half gone
with the high lake level,
stink from the open sewer
of Ashbridge's Bay indescribable
when the wind's blowing right,
litter strewn everywhere, only the trees
seem the same unchanged memory. . . .

And I hear you're married,
have children, so can guess
have lost some of that body
ribbed with such delicate bones;
while I'm also married,
grey hairs showing plainly now,
slightly paunchy and punchy,

and no doubt will learn in time
what lean fare that old bone Nostalgia
is to gnaw on. . . .

EVERY NIGHT A POEM IS MADE

Every night a poem is made
when our bodies fit themselves
in the swaying bucket
of that mysterious well,
bottomless and dark,
where time hangs suspended
on its flimsy cord,
and the sound of the world
is a failing echo.

(Sound of our breathing
trees swaying somewhere
in the neighbour sky).

204

THEIR GUNS ARE POINTED

My darling,
we know they have their wars,
we know they kill with terrible hate in their hearts,
eyes lit with an idiot flame,
the blood of innocents dripping from their hands.

My darling,
sometimes I think their guns are pointing
straight at us, that any moment
we both may be blown into nothingness,

so let us show them we are not afraid,
do the thing we love to do best
right under the cold leering lips of their cannon!

205

MEMORY OF ST. JOHN

(For Kay Smith)

Do streetcars looking like flies
still climb from the docks
up that terrible slope to the Square?

Do the chimes of a certain church
ring the hours the same Sunday mornings
of sober peacefulness, do the gravestones
with centuries' sombred faces
still lean on the hillocks of the park?

Tell me, do those streets still dip and climb
like wild roller-coaster rides, does it rain
as hard as on that night
I hunted Mecklenberg Street
one soaked-through half-hour?

O I wonder if the gulls
hang today in the wash of ships
slipping port? And does the stench
of poverty linger
too strong for even the gusts of storm
from the docks to freshen?

Finally, is there still that uneasiness,
that closeness to evil that comes
at evening when shadows
steal fearless, loom large beneath the lamps?

A Dream that is Dying
(1954)

THESE HOSPITALS

These hospitals—
great high buildings
in which so many die
or lie savouring their pain.

Rilke, *The Notebooks*:
"I have been out. I saw: hospitals.
So then people
do come here in order to live;
I would sooner have thought
one died here. . . ."

Fifty years have gone since,
fifty years of great promise.
Death is not nearly as messy;
cripples, the most grotesque cases,
are kept off the streets or swallowed up
in clean antiseptic corridors.

So you can stroll up the Avenue,
pass by these hospitals, one, two, three of them,
and nothing will disturb the spring for you,
no cries, twisted faces, disagreeable smells. . . .

The rot has been contained,
the windows are high up, the walls are sound-proof,
behind which so many die
or lie savouring their pain.

ANOTHER DAY, ANOTHER DOLLAR

To know that exactly
at six-thirty tomorrow morning
the alarum-clock will ring
(first it whispers, then it shouts);

to see a face (my own)
poised before the mirror,
with razor too far from throat
to do any serious damage
beyond cleavage of stubborn chin hairs;

to taste the breakfast cereal,
the toast, dish of fruit, cup of coffee,
to realize while the last swallow
still sticks in the throat
the clock points toward the door.

Sand-crackling pavements,
autos like obedient puppets,
red caterpillars of streetcars,
faces of fellow passengers
rouged, set hard against the day. . . .

The casual meanness of life
so hung in the balance, found wanting,
at early morning.

THE BIG STREET

Behind all the pyramids
of rainbowed perfumes,
behind all the mannequins
of lifeless animals,

behind all the marquees
of joy and sadness,
behind every shivering
writhing tier of neon,
behind the wild refractions
of a hundred bar-fronts,

a bottomless
boundless pit
of eighty-nine dimensions,
of ninety-eight intensities
of exquisite nothingness.

THE MISER

I'm like a miser who watches
one by one his gold coins roll away
never to return—
                    as these beautiful nights
darken one by one without you
to spend the full purse of their pleasure,
and I imagine there's left for us
only wind, only ice, only snow:

we who nod our heads for the sun to shine,
the rain to cease, the clouds to pass by.

THE CAT

The cat asleep (miracle of shining black),
or waking, stretching the languor from her limbs
like a slowly-coiled spring; or simply staring
sleepy-heavy through those yellow slits of eyes,

is a creature too wonderful, far too wise
for this casual world of floors and beds and stairs,
queen of a kingdom lost now a thousand years,
waiting with infinite patience for its return.

GIRLS PLAYING SOFTBALL

In their slacks which reveal for some
well-curved shapes, others strictly laughable,
in their tight-fitting sweaters
taking every boy's eye
off the game across from them.

They'd like to be ballplayers, though, tough, strong
and swift; their faces beneath the hairdos
are serious, completely absorbed.

But it never quite comes off.
Their voices are a little too high,
the ball never seems to behave properly,
the bats they swing awkward, too heavy:

besides, these bodies were meant
for more spectacular activity
than this game of knock and run
in a dust-blown corner of the park.

TO AN ESCAPIST

You've managed to bury your head
deep enough in your verse.
A major improvement. All that's now showing—
your lyric-dripping arse.

ADVANCE OF AN ARMY

Normandy
summer of that year

Rivers dry
the ground white dust

Dying horses
slaughtered cattle
flies bugs everywhere

Many bodies
of their dead and ours
which wouldn't stop swelling
and bursting the uniforms

With some of our boys
cutting fingers off
just to get a lousy ring.

YOUNG BILL IN BRUSSELS, 1945

Young Bill,
barely ready to shave yet,
right off the farm
and not much with the girls.

In that back-street café
he sat with his buddies,
shoulders stiff,
arms hanging awkwardly
down from his chair.

But the small blond whore
perched on his knee
didn't seem to worry,
one hand on her glass,
the other busy
as a nimble hand could be.

Harry bet Joe
fifty francs then and there
the kid wouldn't tumble,

but an hour later
was still cursing Eve
and her colourful successors,

as young Bill
(all smiles)
disappeared upstairs
for an encore.

NIAGARA-ON-THE-LAKE

Boats today on the river
so many drifting corks,

(or to say it more truly,
so many corked-up bottles),

some gay with children,
happy faces alight,
hands waving to us;

untroubled faces
above the wild eddies,
such innocence
above all that evil

lurking, swirling
beneath the dizzy whirl
seething just below
the shimmering waters;

river devils
spinning their tops
every colour of death,

reaching up at times
almost into the boats

with (or so it seems)
the certain wish

to blot out these faces,
these happy hands
now waving to us.

BECAUSE

Because anyone who kills is not with God,
because anyone who hates is a lost soul,
because our bodies were meant to be whole,
not chopped off at the knee, the shoulder,
by any butcher in any field hospital,

because our children are learning our wickedness,
will carry it with them,

because my country you were never,
are even less now worth all the blood of the young men,
their cries of death drowned out by the cries of drunks and
    whores,
because this war and this world
have made dirty rags of our minds,
once clean, once innocent as white clouds under morning sun,

because of this
we will never know anything more
than a bottomless hunger in our lives,
will run to embrace death with arms of gladness
as he walks to meet us in this blood-stained world.

MECHANICS OF WAR

Guns
tanks
planes

To meet them
men

To join them
death.

217

STUDY: THE BATH

In the dim light
of the bathroom
a woman steps from white tub,
towel around her shoulders.

Drops of water glisten
on her body
from slight buttocks,
neck, tight belly,
fall at intervals
from the slightly plumed
oval of crotch.

The neck bent forward,
eyes collected,
her attention gathered
at the end of fingers,

lovingly removing
dead, flaked skin
from the twin nipples.

218

THE YEARS KEEP WALKING

The years keep walking
with their great piercing cleats
on the upturned faces
of all dead soldiers

spelling out clearly
in blood's strange alphabet

BETRAYED
BETRAYED

THE GULLS: A MEMORY

Night falling with such
raucous racket of bird cries
from crows, robins, starlings
(no sweet singers these!),

that it drove my ear inward,
far backward,
to the seas of fond memory—
St. John, the old wharves,
North Sydney, the fish smells—
but most memorable

that Atlantic mid-March crossing,
the endless zig and zag
of our troopship England-bound,
our sombre escort destroyer
leaving us the second day out,
but the flight of gulls at our stern
not so fickle, but staying on,

hovering, effortlessly sailing
above our propeller's churning,
with easily ten thousand
ancient mariners looking on;

still aloft until darkness
and the time for garbage thrown
out over the side, waiting patiently
for their deep-ocean feast.

But the next morning gone,
not one single wing left
to whiten our wake,

with us all alone now
on that endless emptiness,
no cry but the sound
of our own voice to shake us,
no land ties to guard us
all the long way in
to the fog-ridden,
danger-hidden
legendary shore.

Alone now as death
on that mid-March ocean.

221

PARABLE FOR AN EDITOR

The old car's going fast,
springs just about shot,
the steering a menace
and the less said
about the upholstery
the better.

Get rid of her, Johnny,
sell her for junk
or give her away if you have to.

Don't get yourself killed
taking impossible curves,
or beating a red light.

We need you, Johnny,
we want you to stay alive.

But after all
you've got a mind of your own
and know how to use it.

So all we can really do is warn you.

BUZZ BEURLING

You lived up to the tradition
of legendary heroes
by ingloriously dying
in a second-hand aircraft
of the Jews of Jerusalem.

For one so well trained
in scientific murder
you exited crudely
(for contrast, I imagine,
with the Great Showman
faintly smiling).

I wonder what it was you saw
as you roared toward death,
or if you said anything at all
as you crashed out of this world?

If you did
it would probably be
pure Anglo
unprintable

old screwball.

FOR A MOMENT

For a moment let us forget
that men starve, that men plan killing,
forget everything but this day
of mighty autumn weather.

Let us dream of a world untroubled
as the high blue of the sky,
more beautiful than the maples
flaring on every hill.

O this may be the last autumn
before the unmelting snow,
before our lives are as one
with this lone leaf dropping down to death.

224

NOW GO DOWN

(The Tube, London, 1945)

Now go down
while faces rise
up the escalator,
white, rouged, drawn,
blur of merry-go-round.

Now go down
to tunnel level,
mole entrances,
curved sewers carrying
arms legs bodies
in a tireless flow,
one ebb unending.

Now go down
along platforms electric
into dust, stale air,
tracks laid in darkness,
out of which grinding
your train brakes, pauses.

Now go down
crowded aisle, feel the jerk
as the ride begins,
accelerates, rocks,
lights shaking,
names flashing,
then more dark,
that darkness.

Now go down
into yourself,
holding all nerves taut,
waiting, waiting,
for these doors to open,
to escape to somewhere,
to run forever.

GOD-LIKE

In this room nothing
but dark and our breathing.

We swim, we drown
in the depths of our loving.

I, god of this life,
the mad world's master,

you, warm sun circling
my earth of amazement.

226

FOR WANT OF A LOVER

— fill with delight

Look at her now,
our ravishing Mistress of Poetry—
couched on the great green bed
of this eiderdown country,
soft legs bent
in an invitation to love:

with no-one yet
strong enough
or bold enough
to ride her.

SWAN SONG FOR MY GENERATION

I have watched you all
growing older
(like me)

I have seen you all
getting married
(like me)

I have found you all
writing drivel
(like me)

nicely dead and ready
for history.

THE FLOOD

O lovers
pour your sweat
of the long, breathless nights

on all the hates
on all the small ways of men.

O drown forever
in your flood of loving
these black beetle bugs of evil,
these slimy, squatting toads of death!

228

DEFINITION OF POETRY

Between the books,
between the job
and the baseball games,
between sleep
and walking pavements,

come those few blessed moments
when the pen sings
of idleness
and the heart's simple cunning.

Unsaleable
much-scorned commodity,
cover us all
with your grace,

melt us all
in your fire.

EYES

Eyes
you haven't seen enough,
and yet you're more tired
than a poet's eyes
should ever be.

Instead of deeply drinking
the long cool draught
of trees and grasses,
instead of feasting
on the splashed wild pigments
of girls' upturned faces,
instead of touching
warm darkness of lost streets,
earth-circled blue
and cloud curdle,

you stare too long
above paper-strewn desks
with ink-ants trailing,
all day long the sheer whiteness
of paper mocks you,
each empty sheet a poem
crucified or strayed forever.

Eyes
I'm a coward
eyes
I'm not worthy
eyes
you're wasted in me.

NIGHT SONG FOR DARLINGTON

(June, 1945)

We've missed the last train
with the pubs long closed,
too late for any girls
and our money all gone.

O to be in England
now the last train's gone,
every pub shut tight
and the women gone home.

With our money all gone
and the war over now;
O we've missed the last train
and it's cold in the streets,

with nothing to do
and nowhere to go.
Almost seems we've been here, chum,
many times before.

AIR-FORCE STATION

(East Coast, 1942)

The Group-Captain drunk every night
Rifles carried round the camp
but nobody trusted with bullets
Air crews thoroughly bushed
Our squadron leader daily with the shakes
Four new cases of VD
and the hospital overcrowded now
The Protestant padré is a snob
Watch your feet for broken glass
when you go to shave in the morning
Every hangar window smashed
when that depth charge blew up today
Several deer sighted on the runways
The Group-Captain sloshed in the mess
Coal-gas and sweat in the morning
A sergeant caught using crooked dice
That priest too damned noisy every Sunday
Our rations have been stolen for a year
An airwoman raped last night
Not enough letters from home
Another engine-failure on take-off
German subs up the St. Lawrence
The Group-Captain staggering on parade
Soot on our blankets in the morning....

MY GRANDMOTHER

My grandmother on her bed
struggling for breath,
still sips at life
but would gulp down death.

233

A VERY MERRY CHRISTMAS

On a large fir tree
in the centre of the grounds,
the workmen have hung
many brightly glowing coloured lights,

so the patients looking out
from the high upper windows
can see how inviting
the world outside is—
one great Christmas tree
with the dreams of happy faces
clustering around it.

When the visitors come
with their gaily wrapped gifts,
laughter ripples through the wards,

and it usually takes
the best part of a week
before everyone tires
of this little game,

and the workmen come back,
pull down all the lights
off the large fir tree,
so it stands again naked,
shivering once more
in a world of winters.

234

LA BELLE DAME

O it's not hard to see why these poets
choose the university,
they're clever, they're young and ambitious,
each with the right degree.

O it's not hard to see why these poets
give us so little poetry,
they're nourished, sustained from the dried-up dugs
of the university.

(Seduced by an old bitch they'd probably call
La Belle Dame Sans Merci.)

THE GIRL FROM ENGLISH HARBOUR WEST

... And when he took your arm
to walk you home,
hard, painted girl that you were,

he wanted you again,
and you laughed, you ran
down the road, hell flames
from the open-hearth lighting your face
with the same fiery glow of his desire!

235

HOSPITAL AT NIGHT

The smell here's of death,
white walls the colour of angels,
clean-smelling sheets the shrouds.

I lean out this window,
watch the city below under darkness.
Fifteen floors down the street
alive with people, motors,
lights far as I can see
on a night with a slender, yellow moon.

And suddenly this air I breathe
has a strange, overpowering freshness
that heats the blood in my head,
I am young, I am restless,
my city big, wonderful!

Then I turn away from the window,
talk again to you, or the eyes
of someone I love slowly dying. . . .

236

MUSICMAKERS, NYC

Theirs was almost too good a conspiracy—
the crowd gathered around the two Negroes
(one with guitar, the other strumming with his voice),
still hid the musicians crouched on the pavement,
but had become so large, so noisy,
that the police would soon spot it, break it up—

But while they held forth there was a kind of music
not to be found in any bar or dance-hall,
a music close to the earth, with earth's rhythms,
earth's lustiness.
              The boys were playing
for the money in their hats, of course,
but they'd have played even to themselves for kicks,
for the sheer joy of it.

This was something the cops would soon break up,
but still would go on long after them,
somehow keep flowing, never die.

ON A COOL NIGHT IN OCTOBER

On a cool night in October
two young girls walked slowly
down Jarvis Street.

Not beautiful,
not too clean, dressed shabbily,
hardly anyone looked at them.

But they had to keep walking,
hoping to catch someone's eye,
anyone with a couple of dollars.

There was nowhere else to go.
There was nothing else to do.

238

THE CITY CALLED A QUEEN

How many poems have been smothered
by the tight strangle of buildings,
how many silenced effectively
in the crazed screech of traffic,
and how many more
broken cruelly at the touch
of that slow killer Boredom
(his curse a dark evil mist
over all this city)?

Strange city,
cold, hateful city,
that I still celebrate and love
while out there somewhere
you are carefully working at my death. . . .

239

SEARCHLIGHT AT THE AIR BASE

Here for two years was the centre of our lives,
its rhythms the dying cut, the leaping roar
of engines, its landscape first a length of road
ending at the guardhouse, then crowded hives
of barracks painted uniformly green,
and beyond them glassed boxes of hangars
forever murmurous, great runways ending
where stubby firs hid deer paths, treacherous marsh.

And at night, coming back from town,
happy in the darkness,
we'd leave the highway, turning in to camp,
then see it, watch it flash almost tenderly
in its endless circuit of watchfulness—
our searchlight high in its tower—
sweeping a star-heavy sky with a moon grown cold,
to us a symbol of constancy, beloved guardian
of our youthful dreams, our careless
new-found, exploding strength.

240

THE VOICES

From looking out at too-thick folds of rain
falling intently in vertical weights of gloom,
I turn to see your body naked now,
its whiteness glowing, lighting up this room.

Under the belly's slope the shy, black hair,
above, the breasts small and pointed, with short legs slender
as a deer in High Park: and all of it so clothed
in tenderness, in joy, in breathless wonder,
that suddenly there's no rain or darkness falling,
only the voices of warmth and desire calling.

DIG

Dig, all you poets,
get your fingers working
down into the dirt,
let's see some wear and tear
on those fingernails.

There's life buried under there,
but you've got to work
just to catch a glimpse of it,
you've got to sweat even more
if you hope to capture it,

or even hold it in your hand
for just a moment.

OLD MILL BRIDGE

Under the arch of this bridge twenty years ago
I froze both feet playing hockey
on a five-below winter afternoon.

Now that bridge is still there, only older,
but I don't play hockey any more,
and we haven't had a real cold winter
since the second last year of the War,
while my feet—they could still be frozen
for all they seem to lead me to. . . .

GIRL WITH THE FACE OF SORES

I suppose you might even say
that one could get used to this face
by looking long enough at it.

In time each separate, oozing sore
would develop its own special character,
this red valley full of irritation,
that rounded hilltop of pus.

Even the white skin fighting
a losing battle underneath—one could find there
the eternal parallel—beauty slowly crushed
by relentless ugliness. . . .

But the eyes, it seems, are chicken,
and mostly betray you. And so it's much easier
to turn away, your shame greater than her shame.

242

UPTOWN BRONX EXPRESS

Leaving Times Square,
crowds pressing crowds, descend
the steps, unlock
the turnstile's barrier,
follow feet bodies heads
all swiftly moving
UPTOWN BRONX EXPRESS
to finally stand beside the tunnel's edge,
waiting the low-capped thunder of the train,
the blur of faces, windows sliding by.

Moving aboard hold tightly to swaying strap,
breathe or suck in the heavy air the fans
push slowly, endlessly, watch the local stops flash by,
lights, signs, gates, people, all in a madman's dream

until your station's reached, O blessed number
showing on uprights as the train glides in
to hissing, screeching halt. Then, hurrying up the stairs,
breathe in the air of night, drink in the stars
serene above Manhattan, grave, pitying watchers
of our folly, stern witnesses of this death
millions call life in this lost city of the world.

243

LAST BEER AT THE OXFORD HOTEL

We've drunk our last beer at the Ox, Don;
that old back room where once we drank out of steins
and had to shout to hear ourselves
above all the other shouting, is closed now,
there won't be any more nights like those we knew
before all the gang got killed off or married,
(or worse still, serious and old), when we'd come out the small
    side door
feeling high on two pints of beer,
and head up Bay for the Casino, more than ready
to laugh at the second-rate comics,
cheer and whistle as the strippers came slinking on....

All I know is any beer we drink from here in
won't taste half as good, while our talk
will never be as light, as honest or close again,
not because we've changed that much (we haven't, have we?),
but hell, our old backdrop's been shifted,
the familiar setting axed, and no other place
can ever be the same: we'll sit at a table somewhere else
and feel strange, the beer will somehow taste flat
and we'll wonder why—
                then suddenly
look hard at each other and know.

AMUSEMENT PARK

Everybody likes to see the freaks
grease-smell of uncooked onions
girls of the Moulin Rouge
too fat too old and too bored
the roller-coaster's minor thunder
more grease-and-onions smells
this one lifts weights with his breasts
a large happy crowd tonight
the barker like election time
that old familiar pink-floss candy
the lady's wearing only three gardenias
here here and here
frozen faces on the Rocket
(fun and fear faces)
the mustard perfume of hot dogs
step in closer folks
more screams from the roller-coaster
everybody likes to see the freaks
frenzy colours
light orgasms
that protruding lip of her belly
icecream frejan hamburgers
(Ferris Wheel you Shining Queen)
the girl in the goldfish bowl
grease-smell of uncooked onions
a fine happy crowd tonight
(so tent-like so strange all around us
the impeccable darkness).

245

THE OPENER

From where I was sitting
it looked like an easy double-play.

But at that precise moment
a sloppy-looking freighter
(slipping out through the Western Gap
with a clothesline of washing
half the length of her deck)
glided past the stadium,

and the runner going into second
took one look at that ship
and yelled, "Hey, look, they got
my old lady's black pants
flying up at the masthead."

And when all the infield
turned around to get a gape,
he made second, stole third,
then scored standing up
the winning run in what otherwise
was one of the cleanest-played openers
in a Toronto ballpark.

246

JEANETTE

Jeanette in a fight
calling in boyfriends
to wreck a café,
Jeanette dead drunk
swinging at a cop,
Jeanette on the habit,
riding it up
riding it down,
Jeanette in jail
and out again,
Jeanette on the corner
of Dundas and Jarvis
with the old reliable
merchandise for sale.

One day they'll find her
with a knife in the chest,
or choked to death
by one sheer stocking;

but tonight she's the queen
of this crawling street—
Jeanette with her sweater tight,
proud to show them off
to all the boys—

black hair, big smile,
that's Jeanette.

ALONG THE DANFORTH

This goes on endlessly, it seems,
sad stores, used-car lots, dingy movies,
so many shouting out BARGAINS,
so many fading fast,
long past saving.

People walking the sidewalks
find no wonder in store-fronts
or circuses of neon,

that's why perhaps they all look up
as a streetcar rumbles by,
red flash with its blur of faces,

knowing that these at least
are carried through the heart of this jungle
at thirty, forty miles an hour.

HIGH DIVE

High above, away up there
ninety feet or more,
the barker out front
tells the crowd on the Midway.

High above all the lights,
the snake-lives of people
far below,
        up the swaying thinness
of the tower's steel ladder
he climbs five times daily,
sprightly, as if eager,
as if unable to wait
to stand poised, hardly seen
by the eyes down there waiting
for his slender figure
to fall fall fall
(drum-beat of eternity)
into the flaming pool
(only four feet of water
the barker tells the suckers . . .)

And if some night the wind . . .
a quick carelessness . . .
He'd probably only laugh at this,
saying: that's the chance I take,
and Death, once you've stood
a few nights up here
and laughed at him,
is no longer feared.
Rather, I fear
those eyes below, staring, staring,
those vultures of life
eager to tear my bones,
suck my red blood.

250

RED FRUIT

From lying there on the bed, a light-slumbering cat,
you turn at my coming like petals opening up on a flower.
Sinking down to your warmth of face and arms and hands,
I encounter your lips, red fruit I recklessly devour.

THE BOWLING ALLEY

One person gets a lot of strikes,
another's always on the head-pin,

but whatever we seem to roll,
most of us have that stubborn streak,
keep coming back for more,

taking careful aim,
then letting our ball go
down that long long alley
for the hell of it anyway.

OUR GUN-ARMOURER CORPORAL

Every night our gun-armourer corporal
polishes his shoes lovingly,
though there's mud, two-inch-thick sucking mud
right outside the barrack door,
O shines them till every vein on his forehead
stands out angrily.

Then he sits down, slides both feet in,
carefully laces up, ties each boot just so,
next, slings himself effortlessly up
on his upper-tier bed, where he lies,
clad only in his underwear,
his good shiny boots on his feet.

Now, comfortable at last, quite at ease,
he swallows tablets one by one,
sweating out his final cure
(Lover Boy paying for the love
of a poxed-up Glace Bay girl),

with the glare-heavy barrack lights
catching the immaculate shine
of his twin feet's pride and joy,
even throwing it at times on that face
twisted now in the ecstasy of pain.

PRISONER OF THE STATE, 1951

I'd like to see him strung up,
she says; living in that nut-house
(St. Elizabeth's)
is too damn good for him. . . .

Madam, let me confess
it saddens me to think
so much of the brute
may lie behind the mask
of your passion-flower face,

and perhaps less grievous,
(but more human)
ignorance.

253

ON GRENADIER POND

On Grenadier Pond between the hollows of the hills,
the sail-skaters turn their yellow shields into the wind,
and I forget my half-frozen ears, the ache in my feet,
as my eyes race them over the glare glass, never far behind.

SUMMER'S FLOOD

Caught up in summer's flood I'm lifted
higher than the highest tree, then turned
half-struggling toward the sun,
which pivoting like a flaming searchlight,
enters my brain, sinks into every pore,
melts me, then ladles me
out into the grass, where grasshoppers
dissect my steaming bones.

254

THE TRAIN PAST AUSCHWITZ

"Auschwitz?
Yes, I remember it,
we used to pass it
on the train at night,
and once I noticed
a fiery glow in the sky
and asked some passengers
what it was.
They looked at me strangely,
even for a child,
and said, the concentration camp,
which only left me puzzled
even more than before—
the word meant nothing then."

Fräulein, I long to answer her,
too bad that train didn't stop
right then and there. With the wind
blowing in the right direction,
even you, the twelve-year-old child,
might have smelled what the word means.

CID'S POEM

Nice people, these intellectuals—
when they become tired
of life as it must be lived
they invent fantasies,
or worse, this gathering
in a high loft of a room,
everyone drunk or well on the way to it
with glassfuls of Scotch. And in the centre
a huge, old-fashioned bed, on which
the chorus-girls invited for the evening
take turns with any gentleman
still capable of intercourse.

While all this time the poet
sits gravely in the back kitchen,
arguing with the Negro maid
(almost an intellectual herself)
the pros and cons
of sterilizing the family cat
now curled in the middle of the floor. . . .

ONE OF OUR YOUNG SOLDIERS, DRUNK,
SPENDS HIS FIRST NIGHT IN BRUSSELS

The first girl was a cow,
he reached up and pulled the bell.
The *Madame* sent up another,
also a cow, he almost
pulled the cord off the wall.
The third was very, very young,
small-breasted, not very tall—
it proved no trouble at all. . . .
(He remembered her saying in the night,
"You want maybe marry bee-bee?"
as her hips moved effortlessly,
and he murmuring back, "We'll see.")

Then half-sobered-up in the morning
her beauty seemed a little worn;
and he recalled them kissing madly
after something she'd done—
he barely made it down the hall. . . .

Outside sunlight mounted a wall.

257

FREDERICTON

At last you've visited
"the poet's corner of Canada"—
Bliss, Sir Charles,
and Francis Joseph Sherman,
all born, all Latin'd and Greek'd here.

Not one of them
with very much to say,
but dressing it up, faking it,
so they fooled quite a few in their time.

And it's not hard to understand why.
Outside of her noble-flowing river
this city has little to commend it,
couldn't help but in time drive a man
to drink, or worse still, poetry.

Which vices no doubt are being practised
with the utmost vigour today.

CLUB NIGHT

Knowing if you should look away
even for a moment from your partner,
from the shiny-black surface of the dance-floor,
from the flushed faces in the band,

looking out beyond the music,
to tables close by, the faces at them,
beyond all this to the far corners
of the room, the last tables,

to see there, and there, and there,
lonely eyes, lonely lips, lonely hands,
all echoing emptiness, all breathing sadness,
(moths clinging to summer-evening windows,
breathless, smothered, swept up
in all the glare):
                      look away again,
back to your hand firmly set
on your partner's trim waist,
back to the even beat
of the music, back to all the smiles,
the slight beads of sweat now on the faces,
the beautiful, white faces of the dancers.

RAG-AND-BONES MAN

Maybe if I get it down right this time, O rag-and-bones man,
maybe, just maybe, once and for all
you'll cease to be my all-too-recurrent, crazy nightmare. . . .

London in wartime, the Tube, close to midnight, somewhere
  between Waterloo and Shepherd's Bush,
faces blurred or too clear always entering, leaving,
signs beckoning, lights flashing, doors sliding,
our train gathering speed with coaches rocking, wheels
  screeching high on the turns,
and again the hell of faces ghostly lit, halfway between light
  and darkness,
with me, the strap-hanging airman, still beautiful in beer fog—

then suddenly, at coach's end, you, man or part of a man,
  caricature of something like a human,
wild hair, eyes glazed or not seeing at all, sickly drunk smile
  over pasty face,
cheekbones sticking knife-like through the skin,
skeleton of shoulders holding up a coat or the rags of a coat,
  pockets bulging obscenely,
rags of trousers half-covering spindly legs, toes showing out
  of shoes or shreds of sole and leather—

the whole thing doing a dance, a neck-shaking round, a
  ghostly shuffle,
three steps up, three steps back, the whole body shaking now
  to music leaking out of a long-lost brain,
the grinning faces of the passengers grotesque with the
  ghost-light on them, pale, over-rouged,
but no face matching in any way his own with its mask of pure,
  raptured madness,

and all the time the train roaring on through the earth,
   sliding through its burrow under rivers, rot of cities,
slicing the mole-dark of tunnel, shaking the deepest rat-holes
   of hell,
with always that shuffle at the coach end, that mad, crazy
   dance going on and on,
three steps up, three steps back, dance of death performed
   with all the light-hearted brightness of life,
dance without reason, without end. . . .

Maybe if I get it down right this time, O rag-and-bones man,
maybe if I say it straight enough your dream will fade tonight
   and forever,
maybe I'll sleep with no sweat to soak through my bed, and
   no shaky fear left lurking in the past,
maybe you'll visit me no more, your one and only too-patient,
   long-suffering victim,
O let it be so, rag-and-bones man!

261

ST. MARY'S STREET: 3 AM

(For Louis and Marshall)

The biochemist exhales words which few can swallow,
the professor drones out truths which none will follow,
and on a bushel of talk and a hi-diddle-diddle
sits the Saviour Poet dangerously there in the middle.

THE SNAPSHOT FROM MALLORCA

(For Robert Creeley)

Behind you some hint of water, hills rising
on which houses shelter;
                    but the mind,
easily distracted, returns in an instant
to the face, the beret, and from there
to your eyes:
                 rests there, finally,
falcon by falconer, waiting wrist to tighten,
the hood to rise.

DRUNK, ON CRUTCHES

Simply being drunk
makes it tough enough to get around,
but a guy hobbling on crutches—
how does he figure it at all?

The point I think is
he doesn't: and like this one here
will be doing great if he makes six lampposts
(bet on ten if you must have a sure thing);

which reminds me of horses
and also the plain simple fact
that a horse does much better in this world
than most humans.

Than this one here, this corpse,
this living death coming toward you.

263

HANLAN'S POINT AMUSEMENT PARK

What fascinated in childhood seems trivial or merely puzzling
to us now grown man-size.
                              As I remember
for me it was that magic line of booths
under the Hanlan's Point Stadium
(home of the Maple Leafs when they had real Triple-A
    ball-clubs,
and where, if I can believe him, my father in a bank-league
    game
hit a fence-buster into the bay):
                              here I watched
pink candy-floss spun out, clutched my copper hotly
as I very carefully surveyed the attractions
of the Penny Arcade; admired the more daring
flatten the moving rabbits, the capricious ducks
at the shooting-gallery's clang-clamour; wondered if the
    old lady
in the palmistry booth was a real gypsy or not, what went on
behind the pulled curtain; tried the elusive fish-pond
again and again but never caught anything
but numbers for whistles, cent candy. All the while
the Ferris Wheel continued on up to the sky and back again,
the merry-go-round gave joyous music, and so much
in the warm darkness tingled all around me
with the unknown, the adventurous.

A LETTER FROM MALLORCA

Tomorrow, Bob says,
if there's no wind or rain,
there'll be a bullfight in Palma
(cognac in cafés, ring brilliant
with the sun, bulls charging).

But tomorrow here in Toronto
come wind, rain or what-have-you,
no bullfight, very little cognac,
and certainly no sun strong enough to melt
these hearts, these faces,
chasing like elusive hoops, like giant confetti,
the silver coins, the crumpled bills of their hopes,
down the dust-laden streets,
through the dark, airless office tombs.

FIRST SPRING WORKOUT

Go on, laugh at us if you have to—
we, full-grown men with a bat and a ball
down below on this park grass—
laugh at us till your fat gut aches
so hard you think it's a hernia....

Understand, if you can, though, this isn't our childhood
or young manhood we try to recreate here,
but the very present moment: a simple pleasure
that has us with baseball bats,
not rifles, machine-guns in our hands,
and a new white baseball to throw from glove to glove,
not a hand-grenade to lob overhand at men we've never seen
but which someone has told us are our enemies.

266

VD INSTRUCTION, RCAF

Another precious, sunny morning wasted,
this one spent looking at VD flicks
in a posh new Odeon cinema.
All the grimmest horrors brought to the screen
in breathtaking Technicolour,
no doubt the theory being
that a certain percentage of us airmen assembled
will be too scared now to try sex
with all those nice young (infected) girls
at the local dancehalls and pubs,
(the rest of us were a lost cause
from the very beginning).

Now released outside
into the bright morning Bournemouth sunshine,
every girl we pass
looks so fresh, so soft, so desirable,
that we have to crack wise, whistle after them
in un-airmanlike fashion (much as we will tonight,
hunters on the trail of the hunted,
only then much more poised, much more serious).

So on to lunch now at the Bowling Green,
with the morning lecture fading
and with it all the ugly chancres,
each swollen, dripping penis.
Boys certainly will be boys,
and nothing, nothing stays their heat.

CIVIL DEFENCE

My good friend Homer has returned
from a three-day course on the A-bomb,
and if what he tells me is correct,
when the bombs begin to rain down
there won't be too much point
in running for the family basement.

Which in some ways is almost a relief
after a lifetime in which it seems
there's always been somewhere to head for,
a safe place to hide in.

THE ANGEL OF CHRISTMAS

Saw her today, the Angel of Christmas,
down on the front lawn of the City Hall;

standing beside the thirty-foot daylight brilliance
of the public Christmas-tree, flowing linen
draped round her shoulders the colour of snow
freshly fallen, her black face lit up with such a passion
that the head rocked happily
to the hallelujahs shouting in her heart.

(Crazy old Negro woman babbling to herself,
one of those religious nuts—well, she won't stand there
very long in this cold)—
                    and she was gone
when I came back out of the department-store,
O the Angel of Christmas gone, unloved, unheralded....

DOWNTOWN TV AERIAL

At last a new use
for the TV aerial.

Four and at least twenty black birds
(not blackbirds)
asquat and proclaiming loudly
as their droppings bounce with united splash
off the august roof of the Prince George Hotel.

REVERSAL

(For Avi Boxer)

Ten years ago in our war
we had guns in our hands
and someone to use them on.

But your generation of the Bomb,
bewildered by so many enemies,
has turned the guns upon themselves.

THE RAINBOW

Hung up over Bloor Street
red yellow blue
every colour you could wish for.

But it won't last very long—
not at least
with that pot of gold

at the end of it,
and so many pairs
of filthy hands
wildly grabbing.

OLD MAN LEANING ON A FENCE

I'd hate to be that fence
the old man is leaning on.

Holding up not just
the withered, life-shrivelled,
ready-for-death body,

but the immeasurable weight
of all the wasted, bitter years,
multiplied, grown immense,
crushing the shoulders under.

No fence should be expected
to hold up under that load.

RED BERRIES

This then is you—
one of those large
round, shining,
red-as-flame-is berries,
hanging from the over-
laden bush in the garden;

said to be poisonous,
but so plump, so tempting,
as almost to be worth
the risk of certain death
to bite into deeply,
to stain the teeth once
with that rare, forbidden fruit.

LITTLE MAG

"You are up against
a fossilized orientation
to poetry."
          Yes, and to fight it,
half a hundred bucks and a mimeo,
with from sea unto sea
a tight hostile net
laid between us and the sun.

For What Time Slays
(1955)

POETRY READING

(For Jack Hersh)

Nobody really wants to listen
to anyone but themselves,
and even that is apparently disappointing.

Two go into the next room
where their conspiratorial whispers
rise to loud hisses; all other talk dies
as everyone tries to overhear them.

Another pair leaves by the front door
"for a breath of fresh air"
(they won't go far, it's raining),
while our half-drunk hostess knocks over
another drink in the kitchen
(two down and four to go).

Then by polite agreement
all are silent, even listening
as the boomed bravado of Dylan
commences on the record player.

Not exactly—the professor of English
is searching for an elusive olive
in the lower reaches of his murky Martini.

A BED WITHOUT A WOMAN

A bed without a woman
is a thing of wood and springs,
a pit to roll in with the devil.

But let her body touch its length,
and it becomes a place of singing wonders,
eager springboard to heaven and higher.

And you may join her there
in those hours between sleeping and the dawn.

TWO DEAD ROBINS

In the driveway, their bodies so small
I almost stepped on them, two baby robins,
enormous mouths, bulging eyes, bodies thin wire
stretched over taut skin frames, bones showing
like aroused veins.
                    It looked as though they'd either
tried to fly from the nest above
or the wind had swept them down. For some reason
I couldn't bear to pick them up in my hands,
so got a spade and buried them quickly
at the back of the garden, thinking as I did it

how many will die today, have much worse burial
than these two my shovel mixes under?

THE COLLECTOR

What she collects is men
as a bee honey, leaving out the subtlety
of that swift winger. There's little in the way
her eyes look into theirs *(O take me)*,
her body arches forward *(possess me now)*.

At her age (other women say)
it's so ridiculous: but how much envy
gets mixed in with the fact?
They all say, none, but we know better,
watching their faces closely.

Still, admit, what she collects finally is pain.

GRAN VIA

A gaping wound
in Rosedale's side—
the subway's open cut:

up, down which unwatered
canal of no Venice
the trains shoot on schedule,

gondolierless,
without oars,

in which lovers sit discreetly
as stations flash by,

then kiss almost furtively,
with a certain tenseness,

on the way out the windy exits.

277

BATTLE JACKET

(New York, 1945)

One more of the crowd
that suddenly engulfs this bar
(O cascading juke-box, O poker-faced barkeep!)
on the slum fringe of Harlem,

is a Negro wearing a jacket
on the back of which has been sewn
a huge American flag, and under it
large, picturesque Chinese characters.

The young man is obviously proud
of his green combat jacket,
and no wonder. The inscription on his back
must read something like this:
here is an American soldier,
come to help drive out the invaders,
help him in any way you can.
It doesn't say: this is a son-of-a-bitch Nigger
not worthy to walk on the same side of the street
as another man, so make him feel as inferior,
as miserable as possible, and great will be your reward
in that mighty kingdom of White Skin Supremacy.

Doesn't say it, of course, but might just as well,
(this ain't China, this is the good old USA, black boy).
No, doesn't say it, but you feel it just the same,
up and down this street, in this bar,
along toward midnight now, everyone drinking even harder
to escape the nightmare.

CENTRE ISLAND, LATE SEPTEMBER

(For Gael)

From the ferry-boat see the high green of the park,
no-one at picnic benches, lying under trees.

Here and there a leaf already blown free
by voyageur winds so lustily at work.

Down by the lakefront where sun strikes the athletic cold,
every beach-house is boarded up, all the cottages deserted.

Even out on the breakwall of rocks whose KEEP OFF doesn't
    stop the lovers,
they touch softly rather than kiss, lie apart rather than
    entwined.

Summer's over. Your poet's eyes say it,
that and much more. While your lips make this solemn wish:
"I should like to study surgery in London
before they knock it off the world forever...."

279

CHARLIE

Ten thousand (they say) in the bank,
but still on the corner every day
selling morning, evening papers.

That's my boy Charlie,
almost blind newsvendor.

Counts nickels dimes and quarters
just by the feel of them,
one thick hand making change
like a human coin-machine.

Every once in a while
the cops pick up Charlie,
fine him a hundred
for taking in bets—
just like paying taxes
as the saying goes.

Out in all weather,
his spiel all his own,
more part of this corner
than the weather-grimed buildings,
the street dust, the traffic noise,

that's my boy Charlie,
almost blind newsvendor.

EVENING IN THE SUBURBS

(After Jacques Prévert)

About six he arrives
from a hard day at the office
His dog greets him
his children greet him
even his wife greets him
He sits down
his wife sits down
his children sit down
even his dog sits down
and they eat supper
Then he lights his cigar
reads the evening paper
the sports page
the comics
the markets
Finally gets up
goes into the garden
where he adjusts the sprinkler
then turns the water on
Sits down again
watching the drops
spray through the air
and goes to sleep
quite easily in the deck-chair

When he wakes up
it's dark outside
the sprinkler's been turned off
He lights another cigar
and goes inside
the house seems empty
all the lights are out
Then he remembers
his wife's at the church
his children next door
watching TV
even his dog's gone
He takes a beer
from the refrigerator
but the beer doesn't taste right
He sits down again
in his easy chair
picks up the paper
but his eyes feel tired
he can't be bothered reading
Still he feels like doing something
so he takes the paper
and rips it down the middle
he goes back to the kitchen
and takes the beer bottle
and throws it through the window
his dog coming up from the cellar
gets a quick boot in the rear
Then he feels better
he feels good again
sits down in his chair
falls asleep like a child.

THE MIRACLE

You won't believe it
but I'll tell you anyway—

into his bed at 4 AM
the bitch crawled, rubbed up against him
once or twice, then almost mechanically
delivered five joyous puppies. . . .

And this man of litters,
dreaming of fellowships, anthologies,

woke to a new squeal of Canadiana.

THE LITERARY LIFE

The literary life
and the smell of it,

or the budding young author
up assorted rectums.

Better his mother
should have lifted furniture.

PUT IT ON RECORD

Living so closely
day by day with these people,
I'd begun to think of them
as fine human beings.

But put it on record—
I'm seeing straight again
clear through your filth,
your dirty, lying dreams
of the nightmare dollar.

The pit's at the end
of all you think and do,
and it's deep, it's dark down there,
death dark,

and more crowded all the time.

THE MONKEY, THE ORGAN-GRINDER

The monkey wore a funny coloured hat,
would hop onto the organ-grinder's shoulders,
then down to the ground again. If you had a penny
the monkey would present you with a coloured paper
on which your fortune was printed. All the time
the crank of the hand-organ turned,
the street began to blossom with a music
foreign yet also familiar.
The organ-grinder smiled at you
and patted your head. You would always remember that smile,
you would never forget that monkey.

Both are long gone now, swallowed up easily
by too many years. Would they call the monkey unsanitary,
the music objectionably noisy, if that organ-grinder walked
    today
along this street? Would the children only laugh at him
and his clothes, try to pull the tail of his monkey?
Or would they somehow turn
into the same children we were, clapping their hands
as the monkey takes the banana, peels it cleanly,
and eats it in three gulps?

I can only hope so.

YONGE STREET REOPENING

Hung over Yonge Street today
balloons and many-coloured bunting, a thousand
gay clotheslines across the roadway.

The air is festive, people are almost happy,
so that I rightly wonder: what strange new fever
has attacked my fellow taxpayers, what madness
has melted their icebox hearts?

And I might have guessed it—all the stores
are giving away free balloons, free roses.
That's all it really takes to turn *their* world upside-down.

But the brilliant, high-riding balloons
will make good targets for the kids
and their air-rifles, the long ropes holding up the bunting
good skipping-ropes for the girls.

And the picture I take away—one huge hand reaching out,
straining every muscle to catch in any way possible
a very elusive green mist of falling dollars.

VOLLEYS

1

He has the easy grace
of an Alsatian
mounting a Pekinese.

2

With one hand
picks at his nose,
with the other a poem.

O the virtuosity
the simple charm
of our native poets!

3

Lenin
then Stalin,
now Malenkov.

Lion begat snake

begat pig in trough.

AGAIN THE SANDWICH-BOARD MAN

I know who he is the minute he gets on the train and takes a seat opposite. Short, stubby man with Charlie Chaplin moustache, carrying one of those black bags railwaymen seem to favour.

You're the Sandwich-Board Man, I want to say to him, loud enough so that all the other passengers in the coach can hear—you're the one with the brightly painted face, the long imitation red nose, who strolls up and down Yonge Street every day now, supporting a sign on your shoulders that advertizes businessmen's lunches at a certain midtown hotel. You're the rascal who winks openly at all the pretty girls who pass you, then turns and whistles at a favoured few, making even the longest-faced executive break into a smile as you go through your devilish routine. The same character I once wrote a lousy poem about, one that missed all of your particular magic, your special, wonderful effect on all the people crowding the noon-hour streets.

But instead of exposing him, I keep quiet, watching him very closely instead. However, he's not playing a part now to earn a living, he's strictly on his own time. So I'm slightly disappointed when he continues to sit dully in his seat as the subway stops flash by, looking, acting like any other normal person. And when I come to think of it, why shouldn't he? Who wants to act the fool all the time?

Just the same I continue to watch him closely, not completely certain (in spite of all appearances to the contrary) that at any moment he won't slide one hand along the seat and pinch the well rounded bottom of the woman sitting next to him. And then with almost the very same movement pull an already-lighted cigar from his inside pocket just in time to blow a perfect smoke-screen into the face of the first gallant male coming to the rescue of a very outraged specimen of Toronto's womanhood. . . .

NO ESCAPE

Even down in the subway
you can't escape it—
where to bank your money, what brassière
should cover your true love's breasts,
which cigarette to get lung cancer from. . . .

No escape
until each of our minds
is an endless, flashing billboard
plastered with a million catchwords,
ten million insidious slogans.

And look—up there in the sky
the Hand slowly scrawls
in spirals of smoke
DIE NOW AT HALF THE USUAL PRICE.

THE VOYAGE

(For Martin Gray)

On the seventh day of November
he left Montreal, only passenger
on a ten-thousand tonner
bound for Santiago de Cuba.

Six weeks of blue water,
six weeks between the old
and a new life, six whole weeks
to search inside his heart.

Far behind him Toronto,
that cold jungle city
choking in its dust,
counting its money with one hand,
with the other throwing up
buildings and businesses;
it lay there waiting
for the Exchange to open,
for Sir Ernest to raise his baton,
for the first-period bell to sound. . . .

Before him, what? Warmth, certainly,
of the body and (he hoped) the mind;
time to try his talent without feeling
clocks watched him with their leer,
eyes waited the nervous signal to plead exhaustion. . . .

He'd be lonely, certainly, but loneliness
he'd always known, only this time he'd master him
with all his young strength, make of him a virtue.

And so as Montreal faded
and the great St. Lawrence took them, he went below
to sleep, to dream, feeling somehow that when he woke
the past would have shed itself like an old skin,
lie there at his feet, and kicking it aside,
he'd go above to greet his first new day.

SIXTEEN GRENVILLE STREET

(For Don Owen)

O a room of one's own,
The Cantos
nudging Dante Alighieri.

O a room with a view
of St. Charles' clock-tower
(grey clock, greyer housetops),
of the old man walking his dog
on the roof for its morning pee,
of the woman performing her dance
before an open window.

(With my very first look
I was pushed years back
to University Street,
to that room on the third floor
with the finger of Irving expounding,
with the round joy of Betty's laughter!)

O a room of one's own,
the latest *Poetry* ready
just in case the landlord
forgets to put out toilet-paper,

all within easy walking
of our Bastille of Culture,
of Mallory's English Bar,
of the whores and the CBC!

FIRST SPRING DAY IN THE CANYONS

Even if I were dying
I'd have to struggle up if only for a minute
to stare down Bay Street this fine noon
of April first sunshine. Gape at all the girls
with their high-heel wiggles, their saucy every-colour-
of-the-rainbow coats and hats,
next laugh at all the big shots
carrying their paunches from exclusive clubs,
to waddle curb-side to their long black cars
(thick cigars of success being slowly chewed to death),
then marvel at each Yonge Street store window—
cross-section of all the useless baggage
we burden our lives with till they rebel
(and rightly so)—finally drop a coin or two
in one of the many tin cups the armless, the legless push
    forward,
that and their eyes, spring today bringing out the misfits
as well as all the big and beautiful players
of this whirling game—
                    life, did I hear someone say?

293

FIRST DAY OF THE WORLD SERIES

This morning on Bay Street
a little excitement: a girl
jumped from the fourteenth floor
of a trust company, hit a roof
ten stories below.

She didn't die right away,
she had to suffer a little longer,
even after having made
this supreme, terrible effort.

It seems the human body
is always letting us down
one way or the other.

THE BAR AND THE ALL-NIGHT MISSION

The bar and the all-night mission
are right next door to each other.

Trouble seems to be, though,
the trade is all one way....

TAKING THE CURE

You promised yourself that this evening
would be one of the good ones;
a poem perhaps finished,
one or two letters written,
then a favourite book till midnight.

But there's no poetry in your head,
the letters to friends
pose unanswerable questions,
the titles in the bookcase
call out no invitation.

You end up circling
the room like a caged one,
you finger old magazines
that resist your touch,
even pictures on the wall
fail to soothe or humour.

So breathing almost heavily
you dress, make a point of slamming
the front door behind you.

Then after several blocks
the night receives you,
lovingly, understandingly,
revives you, calms you down,
is somehow one with you.

You walk on, not really seeing
the streets, the windows,
people, anything at all,

just walking,
walking it off,
taking the cure.

THE CHANGES

I can remember when you
were a man we all feared,
jumping up at the sound of your voice, often tortured
by the crazed look in your eyes,
or raked over time and again
by your broadsides, your salvoes of fury.

Meeting you today—now a withered, beaten shell of that
    man—
I understand you so much more,
sense that your bitterness has drained away at last,
leaving you human again, one of us.

And so it does me no good at all
to see death's yellow shadowing your face.

296

MIRA NIGHT

Just to think of that night
makes me twenty-one again.

How the cottage hung
up on the cliffside,
half down to the water,
waters of Mira
rushing down the gorge,
held in the cone
of the moon's cold searchlights.

There were many bottles
on that cottage table,
there were empty bedrooms.
Outside in the night
wild splashing of swimmers,
other wilder noises—
boy-and-girl noises.

We left the wood road
for the darkness of the trees,
did not go far,
lay with pine-needles cushioning
our eager bodies.

O I moved
from the blaze of your lips
to the stoked furnace
of your thighs:
afterward we stayed
a long time listening
to the hammers of our hearts
slowly deadening their sound.

When we came back
there were empty bottles on that table,
all the doors of bedrooms fastened.

No more sounds of swimmers,
no boy, girl laughter,
only the waters of Mira
rushing down the gorge,
caught in the cone
of the moon's cold searchlights.

THE FIRE IN THE TENEMENT

After the fire in the tenement,
beside the four closets of garbage,
six dozen wine bottles, eighteen gas-cookers,
seven wood-burning stoves—

three charred bodies found in a room
which made it a little embarrassing
when not even the landlady
could remember their names.

MADONNA OF THE LUNCH-COUNTER

Such a small girl's face,
such delicate hands
to be serving coffee
at a quick-lunch counter!

What are you doing here
among toothless women,
your freshness somehow smeared
by piles of stained dishes?

Not that we really wish you
anywhere else: for what reason
than to see your face
do we walk these four blocks
(today even in the rain!),
then drink the bitter wash
this place calls coffee,
drink it, then come back
gladly, greedily, for more?

299

VIEWERS

At the moment in this department-store
perhaps 30,000 struggling Christmas shoppers,

and among them these two seated on the floor,
almost smack up against a television screen
which throws the usual line-jumping picture back.

The boy, white, six at the most,
the girl, Negro, maybe five,
their patched clothes needing a wash,
their faces a soaping:
                              now both half-hidden
in a forest of TVs and radios, eyes so intent
on the magic before them..
                              (world to them wonderful
after four in a room, lining up for the toilet,
crowded streets for playing, suppers usually cold).

The salesmen gather round and laugh at them.
God rest you, merry gentlemen.

300

THE FACES OF THE CROWD

The faces of the crowd
turn upward to the window
where she jumped from.

They're waiting for the second act,
for someone else
to make the big leap,

and almost every face
will show disappointment
when it doesn't happen.

301

THE BAT THAT CAME IN ONE NIGHT

Remember in the first year of our marriage
the bat that came in one night?
And the most puzzling part—we never did find out
how it managed somehow to sneak in
with doors locked, screens on all the windows.

Do you remmeber how we both woke up
with this *thing* suddenly flapping in the dark,
and while you jumped muttering from your bed
because something had dared to break your sleep,
I pulled the covers up, and ostrich-like,
covered my head, too startled, too frightened to move.

Then when the lights were all turned on,
our intruder was as suddenly gone,
and all our frenzied search couldn't turn up its hiding-place,
our bat was simply never seen again—

not at least with its crazy, flailing wings,
not with its ugly, narrow eyes,
not with its spider-evil body,

though we've known it here time after time,
an often-calling visitor,
still alive in the flap-fury turmoil of our lives,
still around us in the bat-dark terror of our fears.

WORLD TRAVELLER AT TWENTY-ONE

Caught in the cone of searchlights over Hamburg,
he prayed: Lord, get me out
and I'll make it all up to you. . . .

So the very next night
got stoned in the mess, laid a crying
sixteen-year-old up a Darlington lane.

BRITISH LIBERATION ARMY

Two girls called to us from the doorway
of the café opposite. As we turned to look
both pulled their dresses high above their waist:
in that darkened street white bodies gleamed.

We only laughed and went on.
These girls were learning
but still lacked finesse.
Too bad we couldn't take them
on our next leave to Brussels.
Even whores should be given
every opportunity to improve themselves.

THE NEGRO GIRL

Black, delicate face
among a forest
of pasty-white faces.

Her eyelids closed
for a moment only
as she stood by the door
of the subway car,

and in that instant
my lips had hurdled
the crowd and planted
the warmest of kisses
on those dark, folded petals,

then vanished as quickly
before those quick eyes
could open to discover
her unknown, impetuous,
delirious lover.

304

THE DIFFERENCE

Cold outside and dark.
Somewhere a cat
pleads her hunger,
friendlessness.

One thing which surely marks us
apart from the animals—

man's stubborn pride
more often than not
chokes off his cry.

BOTTLES

If you could pile enough bottles
on this white table-cloth the dancers
as seen through that sea-green barricade
would have the faces of people who are sick,
the unreal creatures of another world.

But you can't: and so the faces
are only white or red-faced, very human-looking,
and it's really you yourself (as you may have suspected),
who has ceased to live,
who wears the mask of one already dead,
who even sits at this table watching the living rotate
to the orchestra's bidding . . .
                              who would love to be asked
to smash these bottles piece by hellish piece.

YOUR ABSENCE

I turn on the light
in our bedroom,
the bed looms up
emptily before me.

Just think
not to feel tonight
the roundness of your body
pressed close to mine
for comfort or for love,
not tonight
or tomorrow's night
(O God knows how many nights!)

I pull back the covers
climb slowly, stiffly in,
but my body's not here,
it's wherever you are,

and my love certainly,
never having left you at all.

306

DEATH BY STREETCAR

The old lady crushed to death by the Bathurst streetcar
had one cent left in her purse when they found her.
Which could mean only one of two things:
either she was very wary of purse-snatchers,
or else all her money was gone.
                                    If the latter,
she must have known her luck would very soon change
for better or for worse. Which this day has decided.

THE CHILD AND THE SNOW

The child can't get his arms around all the snow
though he tries and tries, there's simply too much of it.
So, in the end, he contents himself with a snowball,
smoothing its cold, white roundness in a pleasure of holding
so tightly at last some part of this frozen confection
set adrift and now sifting down
from one of the many far-off
floating ice-cream palaces of heaven.

THE NEW FENCE

("Good fences make good neighbours"—Robert Frost)

Take my next-door neighbour and I,
waiting eight years to put one up,
and now that we've actually done it
wondering why we bothered in the first place.

GIRL AT THE CORNER OF
DUNDAS & ELIZABETH

You want it
or you don't

I'm twenty-one
I ain't
got any time
to waste

You want it
or you don't

Mister
make up your mind

308

LITTER

The uselessness of a man with a pointed stick
picking up waste paper on a windy day!

But not that much more useless than me
cornering, often stabbing wildly
at the thousand pieces of my littered mind,

straining to drop even two or three
into the brown sack of order.

THE WINTER OVERCOAT

For this derelict at least
winter's lasted much too long.
The ragged overcoat he wears
has become some part of his skin,
so he can't shed one without the other.

Here in the desperate blaze
of a noon sun stoking the pavements,
he stands, neither hot nor cold,
neither with or without life, waiting patiently
for the miracle he knows can never happen.

EGG-SHELL BLUE

This is all to their credit—
the Italians in the house three doors down
have painted their house this spring.

Painted it glossy white, with what
I suppose you'd call an egg-shell blue for trim,
that blue uncomfortably out of place
on this sober street, too light, too gay,
too alive a colour for Anglo-Saxon taste. . . .

And who knows?—perhaps only done
to laugh at us gently, to jar us a little,
or much more likely—to remind them
of Palermo by the sea, same blue above,
same shining blue below. . . .

DEAD SQUIRREL

Nothing ever quite so dead
as this squirrel who crawled yesterday
the length of the drive on his belly
before dying in a flowerbed.

His body wet-ruffled from the rain,
while flies crawl over him,
one even lighting in his eye,
the ultimate insult of all.

Yet I still imagine him coming
head-first down the nearest tree-trunk,
or playing at cat-and-mouse
with the old, lazy tom next door,
those electric hops he'd unspring
with quivering tail following,
taking him anywhere
without invitation or a key.

But now nothing ever quite so dead
as this madcap waiting to be covered
with our thin burial-cloth of dirt.

311

PIN-BOY AT THE OLD BOWLING ALLEY

One of the pin-boys
looks more like an ape
than a human.

And some night
when a smart guy out front
hits him bad with a pin flying
from a show-off speed ball,

I wouldn't be surprised
if he came out here fighting mad,
swinging easily along the pipes
below the ceiling,

to drop heavily, clumsily down,
and stare with trembling hands
at his tormentor.

THE RED SASH

The red sash curled
around your slender waist,

a kind of snake
believed neither dangerous
nor venomous,

but being the same
red colour as your lips,

to be handled with care,
a certain delicacy.

WHAT CAN I SAY

What can I say except that they were drunk,
that it was Monday morning—
the day after Sunday,
long, endless Sunday,
boring, restless Sunday.

What more can I say except that the woman
could walk no better than the man,
that they held each other up as they walked,
that the woman took the lighted cigarette
out of the man's mouth, dragged hard on it,
as if that could make everything right again,
which of course it couldn't,
which of course was impossible.

What else can I say except that I felt sick
as they turned out of sight along the little street
leading to the railway tracks,

Which could mean either, I suppose, that I have a weak
    stomach,
or else too much pity to waste on the people of this earth.

314

THE MATING SEASON

Lack of suppleness in his legs
gave them trouble love-making.

What to do?

Why not cut them off
she said, half-joking,
half-seriously.

Which he immediately did.
The fool.

Now in bed
when he inches over with his stumps,
she turns her back on him.

Ugh, she murmurs,
to think that I
with all my beauty
should have ended up marrying a cripple!

THE KINDER DECISION

His first wife, being blind,
mothered him.

She should have been more kind—
smothered him!

315

FLIGHT OF THE ROLLER-COASTER

(Old Sunnyside Beach, Toronto)

Once more around should do it, the man confided . . .

and sure enough, when the roller-coaster reached the peak
of the giant curve above me, shrill screech of its wheels
almost drowned out by the shriller cries of its riders—

instead of the dip, then the plunge with its landslide of screams,
it rose in the air like a movieland magic carpet, some
    wonderful bird,

and without fuss or fanfare swooped slowly above the
    amusement-park,
over Spook's Castle, ice-cream booths, shooting-gallery;
then losing no height made the last yards across the beach,
where its brakeman cucumber-cool in the last seat solemnly
    saluted
a lady about to change to her bathing-suit:

ending up, as many witnesses reported later,
heading leisurely out above the blue lake water,
to disappear all too soon behind a low-flying flight of clouds.

316

CIVIC RECEPTION

At least five tons of ticker-tape
unwinds this noon from Bay Street windows
as a young girl of seventeen
(first to conquer Lake Ontario)
is driven between the hordes
of two hundred thousand
cheering, shrieking Torontonians....

Seeing this can't you just picture
our own triumphal ride
a few years from now—

a tired cleaning-lady
emptying a wastebasket
of torn-up letterheads
out an office window,

while a policeman waits
with a hearty curse
as our 1941 Buick
stalls in the deserted
King and Bay intersection.

317

THE UGLIEST WOMAN

It seems noteworthy to record
that today I saw the ugliest woman
I've ever looked at in my life.

And you might have guessed it—
a man was holding her hand as lovers do,
in fact, looked the happiest person
out walking in the crowds.

And no doubt tonight he'll clamber up
those bulging thighs, board that monstrous stomach,
he her Columbus, she his fabulous
new found land.

THE TOY LADDER

You've bought the bird a toy ladder
to play with in his cage. And now grow annoyed
when he ignores it completely.

But can't you see—
even a bird such as ours, not too clever—
knows after a few ups and downs

there's not too much point in climbing
toward a nowhere that promises nothing.

MAN ON THE BEACH

His stomach in the swimming-trunks sags,
an over-heavy purse, while the sun
is reflected off his round bald head
like hand-mirrors children use
in their happy mischief.

No matter really—
he stands like a boy of twenty
watching the young girls go by
in the flimsiest of swimsuits,
drinking in the lilt of their laughter,
tilt of their firmly-nodding breasts,
gaping in open-eyed wonder
as the pouting sex explodes
in their hips' maddening swaying. . . .

All of this a tonic
no doctor could prescribe. And he wonders,
was it only a dream or did he once walk out
with girls more beautiful, more desirable even?
Finally shakes his head sadly, unable now
after all these years lying buried,
crushed under time's shifting, sifting, grinding sand,

to remember yes or no.

WRITERS' CONFERENCE

It can easily be argued
against the familiar statement
that when writers get together
it's a sheer waste of time.

For what certainly could be more
beneficial, reassuring,
than for one to discover after talking
to a dozen or more of his fellows,

that like him they haven't really written
anything they'd care to talk about
in the last lousy three or four years?

320

THE RECOLLECTION

(For George Nasir)

How best to remember you—
by your words (that methodical cursing
of everything bourgeois or dull),
by your giant, peasant-frame body
moving through dead Toronto streets
in the worst beat-up shoes,
by your nose out-rivalling Cyrano?

Yes, certainly by all of these,
but most of all, I think, by that overpowering
overflowing Red River of garlic
flooding in round the sensitive shores
of my nostrils—
                    you in the midst of it
calmly peeling the wrapper
from another lethal foot of Polish sausage.

THIS SKULL-CAPPED PRIEST

I fear this skull-capped priest.

He tells his viewers
someone must have Authority,

and all too clearly
to even a **fool**
he's thinking of himself.

THE UNCOUTH POEM

Hair colour of the sun,
breasts high and pressing forward
beneath the black-as-death sweater,
hips perhaps a little wide
(after thirty-seven years
and some child-bearing),
under the pants kids wear now.

But more than enough there
that if I could have known her
fifteen years ago,

I'd have lain awake nights
inventing sneaky ways
of removing those pants,
that devil's-own sweater,

(though not necessarily
in that order).

THE NEW MATTRESS

Where once the long valley was
that I rolled quickly down
to the twin towns of your breasts,
to the unpredictable
suburbs of your thighs,

is now a plain
flat and monotonous,
and I don't much like travelling
such usual countryside.

323